MANY STRONG AND
BEAUTIFUL VOICES

MANY STRONG AND BEAUTIFUL VOICES

QUOTATIONS FROM AFRICANS THROUGHOUT THE DIASPORA

By Quinn Eli

RUNNING PRESS
PHILADELPHIA • LONDON

© 1997 by Quinn Eli
All rights reserved under the Pan-American and
International Copyright Conventions

Printed in the United States

*This book may not be reproduced in whole or in
part, in any form or by any means, electronic or
mechanical, including photocopying, recording, or
by any information storage and retrieval system
now known or hereafter invented, without
written permission from the publisher.*

9 8 7 6 5 4 3
Digit on the right indicates number of this printing

Library of Congress Cataloging-in-Publication
Number 97-66638
ISBN 0-7624-0168-0

Cover and interior design by Paul Kepple
Cover and interior illustrations by Charlene Potts
Edited by Gena M. Pearson

This book may be ordered by mail from the
publisher. Please include $2.50 for postage and
handling. *But try your bookstore first!*

Running Press Book Publishers
125 South Twenty-second Street
Philadelphia, Pennsylvania 19103-4399

IN MEMORY OF MY GRANDMOTHER, CLARISSA WASHINGTON,

WHOSE VOICE IS WITH ME STILL.

ACKNOWLEDGEMENTS

Bishop Desmond Tutu says, "In the beginning, God . . . in the end, God." And in the middle was the generous support and encouragement of my friends, colleagues and family, without whom this book could not have been completed. Many thanks, then, to Aja Baxter, Rob Claus, Connie Eli, Jawanza Ali Keita, Sarah Singer, Karen Thompson, Philadelphia Volunteer Lawyers for the Arts, and the resources of Bryn Mawr College. Thanks especially to Frank M. Schneider and Nicole Childers, my research assistants, for helping me to tame the albatross that hung around my neck.

CONTENTS

INTRODUCTION

MY MOTHER RECENTLY JOURNEYED TO Ghana, the Ivory Coast, and other countries in Africa. While she visited she had an experience I've often heard about from other travelers: Her sense of identity was heightened by just standing on the soil where our ancestors were born. She felt deeply connected to the past.

To hear her describe it, mother was transported back in time to the days of the Middle Passage. For a moment, she thought she heard the voices of men and women from the past—reminding her of all that was suffered and sacrificed, and they spoke in celebration and praise of their battles fought and won. They spoke, all at once, of a dream they had for the future: that we make their voices our own, and that we never let our families forget the past.

This book collects the voices of all our families whose heritage begins within the African Diaspora. The term *diaspora* comes from the word *dispersion*. It speaks of any group of people who are scattered throughout the world. More specifically, "Africans throughout the Diaspora" is commonly used when you're referring to people of African descent who are geographically dispersed—through slavery or, more recently, emigration. It implies that although we are black, our values and beliefs are different, and though we live everywhere—in America, in Africa, in Europe, in the Caribbean—we share a history of triumph in the face of adversity.

The speakers in this book come from different backgrounds and professions—they are writers and teachers, lawyers and athletes, doctors and grass-root activists—but they all articulate rarely spoken, heartfelt words. Although their insights are based on different cultural perspectives, they share a common root.

The dictionary tells us that a *taproot* is a main root that grows in a single direction, from which smaller branch-roots spread out. This book is of a similar design. The messages here are exclusively from people of African descent, but each quote travels in vastly different directions, spreading out to encompass the full extent of human experience.

No matter what your background, you'll find something of yourself within these pages. The voices here will blend with your own, to create a vibrant song of peace that endures for generations.

ACTION

THE ROADS FROM THOUGHTFUL CONSIDERATION to necessary action are often bumpy, but traveling them is necessary to resolve difficult problems.

The messages that appear on the following pages emphasize repeatedly that acting with intelligence and responsibility for social change is imperative. According to all the speakers here, the challenge for making a difference in the world involves not allowing your actions to overshadow your reasons or impair your judgement.

Simply do what needs to be done, with secure faith in your own judgment, because doubting yourself is a form of defeat. Roads to change are paved with action—whether it's acting for social change, to preserve family values, or to improve education. Replacing an adversary's negative intentions with your strength of actions says you refuse to let their thoughts determine your course.

The speakers in this chapter share with us the circumstances that jump-started them to act during critical times in their life.

SEIZE THE TIME.

BOBBY SEALE (B. 1937)

American political activist and co-founder of the Black Panther Party

Be responsible with actions, and take responsible actions.

HAKI MADHUBUTI [DON LEE] (B. 1942)

American poet, critic, publisher, and writer

FIND THE GOOD. IT'S ALL AROUND YOU. FIND IT, SHOWCASE IT, AND YOU'LL START BELIEVING IN IT.

JESSE OWENS (1913—1980)

American athlete

I'll tell you why I did all these things. It is very simple. I did all these things because they needed to be done.

MARIE GRACE AUGUSTIN

St. Lucian social activist

We knew we had to take some action, and it had to something stronger than simply speaking out.

SISTER AVA MUHAMMAD

American lawyer

TODAY I TRY TO LIVE A DAY AT A TIME AND DO SOMETHING IN THAT DAY THAT'S POSITIVE.

STANLEY TURRENTINE (B. 1920)

American composer

[T]he more fortunate ones owe it to ourselves and to the world not to despair but to do everything in our power to move the work of human liberation along.

ADAM DAVID MILLER (B. 1922)

American educator

WE MUST ARISE AND GO OVER JORDAN. WE CAN TAKE THE PROMISED LAND.

NANNIE HELEN BURROUGHS (1883—1961)

American educator and social activist

[We must] arise out of the dust and shake ourselves, and throw off that servile fear, that the habit of oppression and bondage trained us up in.

ABSALOM JONES (1746—1818)

American cleric

You cannot have wholeness, you cannot have spiritual well-being or physical well-being in a situation of injustice.

BISHOP DESMOND TUTU (B. 1931)
South African cleric and social activist

Everything that touches your life must be an instrument of your liberation, or you must throw it into the trash can of history.

JOHN HENRIK CLARKE (B. 1915)
American historian and educator

NOTHING SUCCEEDS LIKE SUCCESS.

ALEXANDRE DUMAS, THE ELDER (1802—1870)
French writer

Instead of wallowing in my misery, I just made some changes.

STEPHANIE MILLS (B. 1957)
American singer and actress

Success isn't about walking away. It is about fixing things.

TOMMY FORD (B. T.K.)
American actor

WE LEARN THE ROPE OF LIFE BY UNTYING ITS KNOTS.

JEAN TOOMER (1894—1967)
American poet and writer

EVERY ACTION GENERATES A FORCE OF ENERGY THAT RETURNS TO US IN LIKE KIND.

THELMA COOKE

American executive

A couple of things hurt me: Seeing the homeless curled up in fetal positions as if they're trying to crawl back into their mother's womb. And that if you get a gray hair, you have to quit working. I bleed for the world. If we get a few more bleeders out here, we'll get something done.

PEARL BAILEY (1918—1990)

American singer

I am coming.

GEORGE WASHINGTON CARVER (C. 1864—1943)

American scientist

HORNBLOWERS! BLOW IN UNISON!

UGANDAN PROVERB

I must come out, I must emerge.

RALPH ELLISON (1914—1994)

American writer

I made my speech my birthright . . . talking back became a rite of passage.

BELL HOOKS (B. 1955)

American scholar, social activist, educator and writer

We must always have the three D's: Desire, Dedication, and Determination. We must not let anything turn us aside. And to be truly successful, we must always reach back and try to lift someone else as we climb.

HAZEL B. GARLAND (1913—1988)
American journalist and editor

THERE ARE TWO WAYS OF EXERTING ONE'S STRENGTH: ONE IS PUSHING DOWN, THE OTHER IS PULLING UP.

BOOKER T. WASHINGTON (1856—1915)
American educator, social reformer, and writer

Men and women of ordinary ability become pillars of strength when aroused by desire, stimulated by action.

DENNIS KIMBRO AND NAPOLEON HILL
American scholars and writers

I WAS TO DECLARE THE TRUTH UNTO THE PEOPLE.

SOJOURNER TRUTH (1797—1883)
American abolitionist

It is not enough to express our sympathy by words; we should be ready to crystallize it into actions.

FRANCES E. W. HARPER (1825—1911)
American writer and poet

I'VE NEVER BEEN AFRAID TO SPEAK MY MIND . . . AND I DON'T BACK AWAY FROM THINGS, JUST BECAUSE SOME PEOPLE MIGHT CONSIDER THEM CONTROVERSIAL.

VIVIAN CARTER MASON (1900—1982)

American social worker

By . . . trying to strip off the masks that make people uncomfortable in the midst of chaos, perhaps I can help get things moving.

SHIRLEY CHISHOLM (B. 1924)

American politician and first black congresswoman

YOU'VE GOT TO FIND A WAY TO LET PEOPLE KNOW YOU'RE THERE.

NIKKI GIOVANNI (B. 1943)

American poet, writer, and educator

There's a subliminal comfort in knowing the buck stops with you. You've got to make it or break it . . . I want to leave my children and grandchildren with a mentality that says, "I can fight to get a piece of the American pie."

DOROTHY BRUNSON (B. 1938)

American broadcasting executive

WE HAVE BEEN WORKED, NOW LET US LEARN TO WORK.

BOOKER T. WASHINGTON (1856—1915)

American educator, social reformer, and writer

STAND ON YOUR OWN TWO FEET AND FIGHT LIKE HELL FOR YOUR PLACE IN THE WORLD.

AMY JACQUES GARVEY (1896—1973)

American social activist

I did fight a lot in Karthoum. I was bad. I don't take anything. Sometimes I can say we Dinkas are crazy. That is what I can say. We don't give up. In the United States they call black people nigger, you know, that thing. In my country, the Moslem people call us the *abid* [Arabic for slave]. Really, I don't like. If they say it to somebody, not even me, I fight them.

MANUTE BOL (B. 1963)

Sudanese-born American athlete

I was a tough child. I was too large and too poor to fit in, and I fought back.

ETHEL WATERS (1896— 1977)

American actress and singer

I DID WHAT I HAD TO DO.

HATTIE MCDANIEL (1895—1952)

American actress

Every person is born into the world to do something unique and something distinctive, and if he or she does not do it, it will never be done.

BENJAMIN E. MAYS (1895—1984)

American educator

I've achieved a room of my own—not without determination. One summer I came up here to this room . . . and sat and said I'm not giving up. I threw out the television, which started me down the road to victory.

KRISTIN HUNTER (B. 1931)
American writer

I will. . . . And all that is or ever shall be is but reverberations and repercussions of the first thunderclap. I will. It is both a declaration and a command. It affirms dominion. Take a moment and whisper it to yourself: "I will." Feel the power.

SUSAN L. TAYLOR (B. 1946)
American journalist, writer and editor

OUR PROGRESS HAS NEVER DEPENDED ON THE PRESIDENT OR THE CONGRESS . . . IT HAS ALWAYS DEPENDED ON THE ACTION OF BLACK PEOPLE AND THE POWER OF GOD.

ANDREW YOUNG (B. 1932)
American cleric, civil rights, activist, and politician

CONFIDENCE

FINDING CONFIDENCE IN OURSELVES can be a difficult task, particularly when we are faced with unexpected challenges that we feel ill-prepared to handle.

We may think we're too inexperienced or weak to succeed in a difficult situation. But by believing in ourselves and our own talents, we can find the confidence to organize chaos and to see our way clearly through any situation. Life is a journey, and although potholes and wrong turns can interfere, confidence helps us travel as though our feet had wings.

The talented and accomplished speakers in this chapter believe their successes in life were assured once they developed self-confidence. They have a simple message: Success awaits those who are confident enough to pursue it.

Their voices are not self-congratulatory or arrogant; they simply realized from their own life experiences that self-confidence is the first step toward making dreams come true. Find in their words the inspiration to fulfill your own dreams.

MOTHER'S CREDO: THERE'S NO SUCH WORD AS "CAN'T."

CONSTANCE CLAYTON (B. 1937)
American educator

I cannot read a book but I can read the people.

SOJOURNER TRUTH (1797—1883)
American abolitionist and suffragist

I USED TO WANT THE WORDS "SHE TRIED" ON MY TOMBSTONE. NOW I WANT "SHE DID IT."

KATHERINE DUNHAM (B. 1909)
American dancer and choreographer

All my work is meant to say, "You may encounter defeats, but you must not be defeated."

MAYA ANGELOU (B. 1928)
American poet and writer

Presumption should never make us neglect that which appears easy to us, nor despair make us lose courage at the sight of difficulties.

BENJAMIN BANNEKER (1731—1806)

American mathematician, social activist and astronomer

THE FREE MAN IS THE MAN WITH NO FEARS.

DICK GREGORY (B. 1932)

American comedian and social activist

When I discovered athletics, I found something no one else could ever take from me. . . . Athletics was my flight to freedom.

WILLYE WHITE (B. 1940)

American athlete

I'M LAUGHING TO KEEP FROM DYING.

LANGSTON HUGHES (1902—1967)

American poet and writer

The guy who takes a chance, who walks the line between the known and the unknown, who is unafraid of failure, will succeed.

GORDON PARKS, SR. (B. 1912)

American photographer, filmmaker, and writer

Impossibilities are merely things which we have not yet learned. . . .

CHARLES CHESTNUTT (1858—1932)

American writer

I lived with my fifth-grade teacher for a while. But no matter how bad things got, my mother made it clear that we were not defined by our financial situation. We were defined by our ability to overcome it.

ANNA PEREZ (B. 1951)

American political administrator

DON'T LET ONE CLOSED DOOR STOP YOU.

TERRIE MICHELLE WILLIAMS (B. 1954)

American executive

I have come to believe that until one learns to love and respect oneself, one will not be able to control one's life and destiny. When you have self-esteem, you will not allow anybody to relegate you to poverty or misery or unhappiness.

MAXINE WATERS (B. 1938)

American politician

If you can learn to think big, nothing on earth will keep you from being successful in whatever you choose to do.

BENJAMIN CARSON (B. 1951)

American physician

Self-mastery begins with making your intentions clear and understanding that the only limitations are those we devise in our mind.

SUSAN L. TAYLOR (B. 1946)

American journalist, writer and editor

I don't think I was courageous. I think I was determined.

DAISY BATES (B. 1914)

American journalist and editor

IF YOU CAN'T RUN, WALK. IF YOU CAN'T WALK, CRAWL. BUT BY ALL MEANS, KEEP MOVING.

MARTIN LUTHER KING, JR. (1929–1968)

American cleric, civil rights leader, and writer

YOU GOT TO WALK THAT LONESOME VALLEY, YOU GOT TO WALK IT FOR YOURSELF. NOBODY HERE CAN WALK IT FOR YOU, YOU GOT TO WALK IT FOR YOURSELF.

AFRICAN AMERICAN SPIRITUAL

[B]e about something useful.

CORA CATHERINE CALHOUN HORNE (1865–1932)

American suffragist and social worker

Self reliance is the fine road to independence.

MARY ANN SHADD (1823–1893)

American journalist and educator

SELF-HELP IS THE BEST HELP.

AESOP (620 B.C.–560 B.C.)

African storyteller

LEARN TO RECOGNIZE YOUR GOD-GIVEN TALENTS (AND WE ALL HAVE THEM). DEVELOP THESE TALENTS AND USE THEM IN THE CAREER YOU CHOOSE.

BENJAMIN CARSON (B. 1951)

American physician

The biggest mistake most people make is to want to become something before they are something. You first have to be something and be it whole-heartedly, and then you can become what you want.

PEARL BAILEY (1918—1990)

American singer

I know that there might be people better than me, but I just have confidence in myself.

CHRIS WEBBER (B. 1973)

American athlete

IF YOU DON'T HAVE CONFIDENCE, YOU'LL ALWAYS FIND A WAY NOT TO WIN.

CARL LEWIS (B. 1961)

American athlete

[T]he mind is a powerful thing. From the tip of my toes to the last hair on my head, I had complete confidence.

JOE LOUIS (1914—1981)

American athlete

always had confidence. It came because I have lots of initiative. I wanted to make something of myself.

EDDIE MURPHY (B. 1961)

American entertainer

I never ran my train off the track and I never lost a passenger.

HARRIET TUBMAN (1820—1913)

American abolitionist

[I]F YOU HAVE A PURPOSE IN WHICH YOU CAN BELIEVE, THERE'S NO END TO THE AMOUNT OF THINGS YOU CAN ACCOMPLISH.

MARIAN ANDERSON (1902—1993)

American singer

I felt so tall within, I felt the power of a nation within me.

SOJOURNER TRUTH (1797—1883)

American abolitionist

No one need fear death. We need fear only that we may die without having known our greatest power.

NORMAN COUSINS

American writer

I AM THE GREATEST.

MUHAMMAD ALI (B. 1942)

American athlete

I GO EVERYWHERE WITHOUT HESITATION. HALLELUJAH!

VIRGINIA BRINDIS DE SALAS

Uruguayan poet

Human[s] have value and power to determine what happens. People who think they're victims haven't come to grips with their own power.

MAXINE WATERS (B. 1938)

American politician

NO ONE CAN DUB YOU WITH DIGNITY. THAT'S YOURS TO CLAIM.

ODETTA (B. 1930)

American singer

I tell my children. Never use the words, "I can't." Say, "I'll try."

RUBY MIDDLETON FORSYTHE

American educator

[I] don't believe we will produce strong soldiers by moaning about what the enemy has done.

JESSE JACKSON (B. 1941)

American cleric and civil rights leader

The most potent weapon in the hands of the oppressor is the mind of the oppressed.

STEVEN BIKO (1946—1977)

South African political activist

Nothing in the universe is attained by doing nothing. You must always give up something to get something. It's extremely basic, you can't fill a cup without giving up its contents first. You can't even move to a new place in the room without giving up the space you occupy. In other words sacrifice is a basic concept of our universe.

TRADITIONAL AFRO-CUBAN RITE

We are numerous enough, and all we need is to be intelligent enough to take care of ourselves.

P. B. S. PINCHBACK (1837—1921)
American politician

I GOT MYSELF A START BY GIVING MYSELF A START.

MADAME C. J. WALKER (1867—1919)
American entrepreneur and beautician

From my early childhood, they taught me a whole range of skills from carpentry to painting. My father always insisted I learn how to work on cars. His notion was that if I could do a transmission job, I could make my living anywhere in the world.

JENNIFER LAWSON (B. 1946)
American executive

I'M INDEPENDENT, YOU COULD SAY, BY CHOICE.

BILL WHITE (B. 1934)
American athlete and artist

THE STORY I HAVE, NOBODY COULD STEAL.

DOUG WILLIAMS (B. 1955)

American athlete

You can focus on the obstacles, or you can go on and decide what you do about it. To me, it breaks down to that: you can do and not just be.

GLORIA DEAN RANDLE SCOTT (B. 1938)

American educator

So many great opportunities are open to you—grasp, hold, and by all means make the most of them. If one door closes in your face, try another. The size of your life is determined by the size of your plans. Utilize what you have learned. If given the tools, use time wisely and carve a place for yourself in this big world.

CHRISTINA FORTE (B. 1906)

American writer

Don't let anything stop you. There will be times when you'll be disappointed, but you can't stop. Make yourself the best that you can make out of what you are. The very best.

SADIE TANNER MOSSELL ALEXANDER (1898—1989)

American scholar

There is strength beyond our strength, giving strength to our strength.

HOWARD THURMAN (1900—1981)

American theologian, educator, and writer

GRAY SKIES ARE JUST CLOUDS PASSING OVER.
EDWARD KENNEDY "DUKE" ELLINGTON (1894—1974)
American composer and bandleader

It's time to bring down the volume and bring up the program.
AL SHARPTON (B. 1955)
American cleric and social activist

I AM SICK AND TIRED OF BEING SICK AND TIRED.
FANNIE LOU HAMER (1917—1977)
American civil rights activist

We cannot think of uniting with others, until after we have first united among ourselves. We cannot think of being acceptable to others until we have first proven acceptable to ourselves.
EL-HAJJ MALIK EL-SHABAZZ [MALCOLM X] (1925—1965)
American cleric and political activist

CAN'T NOTHIN' MAKE YOUR LIFE WORK IF YOU AIN'T THE ARCHITECT.
TERRY MCMILLAN (B. 1951)
American writer

What makes you think the world owes you something?
GWENDOLYN BROOKS (B. 1917)
American poet and educator

CREATIVITY

CREATIVITY ISN'T A QUALITY POSSESSED only by artists. Rather it's the most essential ingredient in a meaningful and fulfilling life. The speakers here encourage us to look for wonder, color, and beauty, with the keen eye of an artist, and to celebrate those qualities of life in the we way live. Indeed, our lives are a work of art.

It may be said that art and politics are intertwined. Within these pages, a number of voices debate the role of artists in society. While some think it's necessary that artists apply their creativity to social change, most concentrate on the role of creative expression as a means of self-discovery. Learning to view ourselves as works of art—or, perhaps, works in progress—is the dominant message of this chapter. It's a message that can never be delivered too often to those among us who can see little beauty in our surroundings and circumstances.

The qualities that make an artist—passion, vision, an unerring sense of style, a determination to breathe life into a world grown old and stale—are not limited to those who wield a paint brush, a pen, or a camera. Anyone can possess an artist's imagination. We're challenged to approach everything about our lives with a creative spark.

THE ESSENCE OF LIFE IS IN CREATIVITY; THAT IS MAN'S INHERENT SEXUALITY IN HIS ROMANCE WITH NATURE.

SANDRA BETH WILLIAMS (B. 1948)

American dancer

If one is obsessed, perhaps demonic, in his effort to create and to create anew, the rewards are manifold.

CHARLES GORDONE (B. 1925)

American actor

There are three things I was born with in this world, and there are three things I will have until the day I die: hope, determination, and song.

MIRIAM MAKEBA (B. 1932)

South African singer

I learned a long time ago that self-dignity and racial pride could be consciously approached through art.

JOHN T. BIGGERS (B. 1924)
American artist

LIFE AND ART ARE INTERRELATED. FOR MAN IS THE PRODUCT OF HIS CULTURE, AND THEREFORE HIS ART HELPS TO MOLD HIS TOTAL DEVELOPMENT.

EUGENE PERKINS (B. 1932)
American artist

True art always comes from cultural necessity.

ELIZABETH CATLETT (B. 1915)
American artist

ART . . . REACTS TO OR REFLECTS THE CULTURE IT SPRINGS FROM.

SONIA SANCHEZ (B. 1934)
American poet and educator

Art is not living. It is the use of living.

AUDRE LORDE (1934—1992)
American poet and writer

CEASE TO BE A DRUDGE, SEEK TO BE AN ARTIST.

MARY MCLEOD BETHUNE (1875—1955)
American educator, civil rights leader, and co-founder of Bethune-Cookman College

I don't understand art for art's sake. Art is the guts of the people.

ELMA LEWIS (B. 1921)

American artist

THE FUNCTION OF ART IS TO DO MORE THAN TELL IT LIKE IT IS—IT'S TO IMAGINE WHAT IS POSSIBLE.

BELL HOOKS (B. 1955)

American writer and educator

Art is a way of processing destiny.

MARVIN GAYE (1939—1984)

American singer and composer

I SUPPOSE I THINK THAT THE HIGHEST GIFT THAT MAN HAS IS ART AND I AM AUDACIOUS ENOUGH TO THINK OF MYSELF AS AN ARTIST—THAT THERE IS ... JOY AND BEAUTY AND ILLUM-INATION AND COMMUNION BETWEEN PEOPLE TO BE ACHIEVED THROUGH THE DISSECTION OF PERSONALITY.

LORRAINE HANSBERRY (1930—1965)

American playwright

Art is a moral power ... revealing to us a glimpse of the absolute ideal of perfect harmony.

EDWARD MITCHELL BANNISTER (1828—1901)

Canadian-born American artist

THE TRUE WORK OF ART IS A CREATION NOT OF THE HANDS BUT OF THE MIND AND SOUL OF THE ARTIST.

NANCY ELIZABETH PROPHET (1890—1960)

American artist

I shall dance all my life, I was born to dance, just for that. To live is to dance, I would like to die, breathless, spent, at the end of a dance.

JOSEPHINE BAKER (1906—1975)

American-born French entertainer

I do not consider it derogatory, my friends, for persons to live out to service . . . and I would highly commend the performance of almost anything for an honest livelihood.

MARIA W. STEWART (1803—1879)

American abolitionist and educator

THERE IS HARDLY ANY MONEY INTEREST IN THE REALM OF ART, AND MUSIC WILL BE HERE WHEN MONEY IS GONE.

LOUIS "SATCHMO" ARMSTRONG (1900—1971)

American musician, composer, and bandleader

To work with your hands is to feed your own mouth and maybe your neighbor's. To work with the mind is to unleash the feet of millions.

JOSEPH SEAMON COTTER, SR. (1861—1949)

American poet and playwright

You should always know when you're shifting gears in life. You should leave your era, it should never leave you.

LEONTYNE PRICE (B. 1927)

American singer

OPPOSITION IS THE LIFE OF AN ENTERPRISE; CRITICISM TELLS YOU THAT YOU ARE DOING SOMETHING.

PAULINE ELIZABETH HOPKINS (1859—1930)

American writer

Making the simple complicated is commonplace; making the complicated simple, awesomely simple, that's creativity.

CHARLES MINGUS (1922—1979)

American musician and composer

I want the ordinary person to be able to relate to what I'm doing. Working, figuratively, is the dues I must want, and am privileged to pay so that ordinary people can relate to my work and not get lost trying to figure out what it means.

ELIZABETH CATLETT (B. 1915)

American artist

I DON'T DESIGN CLOTHES FOR THE QUEEN, BUT FOR THE PEOPLE WHO WAVE AT HER AS SHE GOES BY.

WILLI SMITH (1948—1987)

American fashion designer

THERE IS A SOCIAL AND POLITICAL CONSEQUENCE TO EVERY-THING I DO . . . I THINK TOO OFTEN AN AMERICAN AESTHETIC USES AS ITS BASE WESTERN EUROPEAN THEATER. THE AMERICAN THEATER WILL ONLY COME FROM AN AESTHETIC THAT TAKES FROM ALL THE VARIOUS CULTURAL INFLUENCES—NATIVE AND MINORITY.

LLOYD RICHARDS (B. 1919)

Canadian theater director

Man's highest aspirations come from nature. A world without color would seem dead. Color is life. Light is the mother of color. Light reveals to us the spirit and living soul of the world through colors.

ALMA THOMAS (1891—1978)

American artist

I CREATE FROM THE RHYTHMIC-COLOR-RAPPING LIFESTYLE OF BLACK FOLK.

NELSON STEVENS (B. 1938)

American artist and educator

I had been forced to spend my whole lifetime discussing the implications of color. . . . This was to me a waste of time, and whatever talent I had . . . the opportunities I really wanted were closed to me.

ANNA ARNOLD HEDGEMANN (1899—1990)

American educator and civil rights activist

I never drew a decent thing until I felt the rhythm of New York . . . as distinct as the human heart. And I'm trying to put it on canvas.

BEAUFORD DELANEY (1902—1979)

American artist

I LOVE TO PAINT. IT NOURISHES MY SOUL AS FOOD NOURISHES THE BODY. IF I CREATE SOMETHING BEAUTIFUL WHICH ENRICHES THE LIVES OF OTHERS, THEN MY ART SERVES A DUAL PURPOSE.

ALICE TAYLOR GAFFORD (1886—1981)

American artist

I have always wanted my art to service Black people—to reflect us, to relate to us, to stimulate us, to make us aware of our own potential.

SAMELLA LEWIS (B. 1924)

American artist, educator, and writer

There are few things that express the mood of the Negro better than his humor.

SIDNEY POITIER (B. 1924)

American actor

I SAW . . . I COULD DO A HELLUVA LOT MORE FOR BLACKS BY BEING A BLACK ARTIST RATHER THAN A BLACK ACTIVIST.

PAUL WINFIELD (B. 1940)

American actor

The newfound pleasure in doing something worthwhile is quite sufficient as a motive . . . to keep things going.

JOSEPHINE BEALL WILSON BRUCE (1853—1923)

American educator

WE ALL HAVE HAD SOMETHING IN MIND AND WE DIDN'T WANT TO TALK ABOUT IT TO ANYBODY, BUT THE BURDEN IS REAL HEAVY UNTIL YOU COULD MAKE SOME KINDA SOUND ABOUT IT, YOU COULD EXPRESS YOURSELF TO SOMEBODY, SORT OF LIGHTEN THINGS UP.

HENRY TOWNSHEND

American musician

I have created nothing really beautiful, really lasting, but if I can inspire . . . youngsters to develop the talent I know they possess, then my monument will be in their work.

AUGUSTA SAVAGE (1892—1962)

American artist

WE WERE FREE . . . EVEN IF WE DID NOT HAVE MUCH MATERIALLY. WE HAD TIME TO SIT DOWN AND TALK FOR HOURS. THAT WAS WHY WE WERE THERE, TO EXPRESS OURSELVES FREELY.

HERBERT GENTRY (B. 1919)

American artist

I consider writing and important arm of the Black liberation movement and of the struggles of all peoples for liberation.

ERNEST DANIEL KAISER (B. 1915)
American editor and bibliographer

Writing is both an obsessive struggle for recognition and a futile attempt to exorcise the vague anguish that mocks every pursuit.

THELMA STILES (B. 1939)
American editor and writer

THE ABILITY TO TALK IS POWER. I LEARNED THAT VERY YOUNG, THAT THE PEOPLE WHO COULD RAP AND WRITE, YOU DIDN'T HAVE TO FIGHT THAT MUCH. YOU KNOW, IT WAS MY WEAPON.

ETHERIDGE KNIGHT (1931—1991)
American poet and writer

I always identified with orphans. Young people alone by themselves in society . . . the things that have happened to me, the things I've seen: children who were abused, children who couldn't walk or talk, children who were taken in to do housework . . . I wrote to incorporate the thing I was learning.

ROSA CUTHBERT GUY (B. 1925)
American writer

[W]RITE ABOUT WHAT YOU KNOW BEST.

WALTER MOSELY (B. 1952)
American writer

Very early in life I became fascinated with the wonders language can achieve.

GWENDOLYN BROOKS (B. 1917)
American poet and educator

WHEN I'M CARRYING A STORY AROUND IN MY HEAD, I FEEL AS IF I'M HOLDING MY HEAD FUNNY. SOMETIMES I WANT TO EXPLAIN TO PEOPLE ON THE STREET THAT I'M JUST TRYING TO KEEP THE WORDS FROM SPILLING OUT UNTIL I GET TO A QUIET PLACE WITH PEN AND PAPER.

ELOISE GREENFIELD (B. 1929)
American writer

I've got this ability to make something out of nothing. I can clap my hands and make magic.

BILL T. JONES (B. 1952)
American dancer and choreographer

I'm always on the search for a fresh concept.

LIONEL HAMPTON (B. 1909)
American musician and bandleader

I AM NOT A SPECIAL PERSON. I AM A REGULAR PERSON WHO DOES SPECIAL THINGS.

SARAH VAUGHAN (1924—1990)
American singer

A LEGEND IS AN OLD MAN WITH A CANE KNOWN FOR WHAT HE USED TO DO. I'M STILL DOING IT.

MILES DAVIS (1926—1991)
American musician and composer

As for the hard times I've had—I've never been jealous of any musician, or anything. Musicians and other people have told lies on me, sure, and it has kept me from jobs for a while. . . . But it don't bother me. I kept on making it—recording and doing what I'm doing, and thinking. While they were talking, I was thinking music and still trying to play.

THELONIOUS MONK (1917—1992)
American musician and composer

Jazz is . . . the sensuousness of romance in our dialect.

WYNTON MARSALIS (B. 1961)
American musician and composer

I JUST SIT, WINK, AND PLAY.

WILLIAM "COUNT" BASIE (1904—1984)
American composer and musician

Music is your own experience, your thoughts, your wisdom. If you don't love it, it won't come out your horn.

CHARLIE "BIRD" PARKER (1920—1955)
American musician and composer

THE BLUES WAS LIKE A PROBLEM CHILD THAT YOU MAY HAVE HAD IN THE FAMILY. YOU WAS A LITTLE BIT ASHAMED TO LET ANY-BODY SEE HIM, BUT YOU LOVED HIM.

RILEY "B. B." KING (B. 1925)

American musician and composer

What is soul? It's like electricity—we don't really know what it is, but it's a force that can light a room.

RAY CHARLES (B. 1930)

American musician and composer

[E]very note that I play, every song that I've ever worked on is really from the people.

HUGH MASEKELA (B. 1939)

American musician

GUESS ALL SONGS IS FOLK SONGS. I NEVER HEARD NO HORSE SING 'EM.

"BIG BILL" BROONZY (1893—1958)

American musician

Songs are more than rhymes. Songs need a beginning, middle, and end. Like a story.

BERRY GORDY, JR. (B. 1929)

American entrepreneur and founder of Motown Records

Rhythm is the element that infuses music with a biological force that brings forth a psychological truth.

FRANCES BEBEY (B. 1929)

Cameroonian musicologist and writer

GOING ON STAGE TO SING IS LIKE STEPPING INTO A PERFECT WORLD. THE PAST MEANS NOTHING. WORRIES ABOUT THE FUTURE DO NOT EXIST. ALL THAT MATTERS IS THE MUSIC.... THERE IS NO ONE PLACE WHERE I AM MOST AT HOME, WHERE THERE IS NO EXILE.

MIRIAM MAKEBA (B. 1932)

South African singer

Music is born with each child and accompanies him throughout life.

FRANCES BEBEY (B. 1929)

Cameroonian musicologist and writer

DREAMS

THE CAPACITY TO CONTINUE DREAMING, even in the face of adversity, makes even the hardest times somehow easier to bear.

Long after his famous "I Have a Dream" speech, Dr. Martin Luther King declared that he still had a dream, and with those words he encouraged us all to hold on to our own dreams. For Dr. King and countless others, dreams mean hope. If we can hope, then we are most certainly alive.

Hope motivates us to find the strength to endure through strife, and to reach for things that seem almost impossible. Within this chapter, entertainers and athletes, writers and scholars speak of their achievements—of the heights to which they've climbed. Their success is tangible evidence that dreams are attainable.

Dreams are visual, vibrant, colorful scenarios that take place in our mind's eye. All the speakers in this chapter make a connection between dreaming and seeing. They all encourage us to use dreams as a way of reaching for those things we can spy on the horizon, but are just out of our grasp.

YES, I AM PERSONALLY THE VICTIM OF DEFERRED DREAMS, OF BLASTED HOPES, BUT IN SPITE OF THAT I CLOSE TODAY BY SAYING I STILL HAVE A DREAM, BECAUSE, YOU KNOW, YOU CAN'T GIVE UP IN LIFE. IF YOU LOSE HOPE, SOMEHOW YOU LOSE THE VITALITY THAT KEEPS LIFE MOVING, YOU LOSE THE COURAGE TO BE, AND THE QUALITY THAT HELPS YOU GO ON IN SPITE OF IT ALL. AND SO TODAY, I STILL HAVE A DREAM.

MARTIN LUTHER KING, JR. (1929—1968)
American cleric, civil rights leader, and writer

I want to see how life can triumph.

ROMARE BEARDEN (1914—1918)
American artist

I am where I am because I believe in all possibilities.

WHOOPI GOLDBERG (B. 1955)
American comedian and actress

THE MORE YOU PRAISE AND CELEBRATE IN LIFE, THE MORE THERE IS IN LIFE TO CELEBRATE.

OPRAH WINFREY (B. 1954)

American broadcaster and actress

I believe in the American proposition, the American Dream, because I've seen it in my own life.

CLARENCE THOMAS (B. 1948)

American Supreme Court Justice

WE MUST TEACH OUR KIDS TO DREAM WITH THEIR EYES OPEN.

HARRY EDWARDS (B. 1942)

American sociologist

Without life, there is nothing.

ZULU PROVERB

[I] believe in hearing the inaudible and touching the intangible and seeing the invisible.

ADAM CLAYTON POWELL, JR. (1908—1972)

American cleric, politician, and civil rights leader

WE SPECIALIZE IN THE WHOLLY IMPOSSIBLE.

NANNIE HELEN BURROUGHS (1879—1961)

American educator and social activist

THE DREAM IS REAL, MY FRIENDS. THE FAILURE TO MAKE IT WORK IS THE UNREALITY.

TONI CADE BAMBARA (1939—1995)

American writer

If one is lucky, a solitary fantasy can totally transform a million realities.

MAYA ANGELOU (B. 1928)

American poet and writer

[O]ppression . . . can rob people of their will to try, and make them take themselves out of the running of life.

JOHNETTA COLE (B. 1936)

American educator and president of Spellman College

I DARE NOT FAIL.

MARIA LOUISE BALDWIN (1856—1922)

American educator

No person has the right to rain on your dreams.

MARIAN WRIGHT EDELMAN (B. 1939)

American attorney and founder of the Children's Defense League

NOBODY'S GOING TO RAIN ON MY PARADE, INCLUDING ME.

HALLIE BEACHEM BROOKS (1907—1985)

American librarian

I'm not disgusted. I'm not deterred. I understand power, and I know what can be done.

MAXINE WATERS (B. 1938)

American politician

I refuse to let my nation's fixation with color deter me from fulfilling myself.

BERNARD SHAW (B. 1940)

American broadcast journalist

[I] AM NOT A QUITTER. I WILL FIGHT UNTIL I DROP. THAT IS A STRENGTH THAT IS IN MY SINEW. . . . IT IS A MATTER OF HAVING SOME FAITH IN THE FACT THAT AS LONG AS YOU'RE ABLE TO DRAW BREATH IN THE UNIVERSE YOU HAVE A CHANCE.

CICELY TYSON (B. 1942)

American actress

You have to know you can win. You have to think you can win. You have to feel you can win.

"SUGAR" RAY LEONARD (B. 1956)

American athlete

LOSE NOT COURAGE, LOSE NOT FAITH, GO FORWARD.

MARCUS GARVEY (1887—1940)

Jamaican social activist

I TELL [KIDS] THEY DON'T HAVE TO BE AN ATHLETE TO ACQUIRE SELF-IMAGE. BE WHAT YOU ARE. WRITER. STUDENT. LET IT HAPPEN, AND DRAW OFF THAT.

JASMINE GUY (B. 1964)

American actress

If you don't read, you can't write, and if you can't write, you can stop dreaming.

CARL THOMAS ROWAN (B. 1925)

American journalist

What I dream of is changing the image held by the children. We have made them believe that everything beautiful is outside the community. I want them to make beauty in this community.

DOROTHY LEIGH MAYNOR (B. 1910)

American singer

I want my words to have an educational function.

YOUSSOU N'DOUR (B. 1959)

Senegalese singer, composer, and drummer

I'M INSPIRED WHEN I WALK DOWN THE STREET AND STILL SEE PEOPLE TRYING. A LOT OF THEM LOOK AS IF THEY'RE ON THEIR LAST LEG, BUT THEY'RE STILL GETTING UP SOMEHOW.

FAITH RINGGOLD (B. 1934)

American artist

FACED WITH THE STRUGGLE OF overcoming adversity, there are many speakers in this book who argue that action balanced by reason is the most successful action of all. And in this chapter, that message becomes a little more fine-tuned. The speakers here insist that no struggle will succeed if you rely too much on emotion and not enough on education.

Learning is power. The important thing is to set goals, study the strategy of those who have achieved success, and tailor that strategy to your own personality and temperament. If we fail to learn from what others have achieved then we will also fail to see what sort of contribution remains to be made. Ignoring the past means we are doomed to repeating it.

Without fanfare or conceit, the speakers here present themselves as educators, offering to share the lessons they have learned about life with others. They do this because they recognize the role of education in a person's success, and because they know that teaching about the past lays the groundwork for a successful future.

THE LACK OF KNOWLEDGE IS DARKER THAN THE NIGHT.
AFRICAN PROVERB

Knowledge is power.
KIKUYU PROVERB

Whoever works without knowledge works uselessly.
AFRICAN PROVERB

POWER IS WHEN I WALK INTO THIS SCHOOL AND THESE LITTLE KIDS' EYES HOLD WONDER WITH A CUP.
MARVA NETTLES COLLINS (B. 1936)
American educator

Mastery of language affords remarkable power.
FRANTZ FANON (1925—1961)
Martiniquan-born Algerian psychiatrist and writer

LANGUAGE IS [AN] OCCUPATION. . . .

CHRISTOPHER GILBERT

American poet and writer

Nothing is more powerful and liberating than education.

WILLIAM GRAY (B. 1941)

American politician and president of UNCF

Only extensive education, continued wise government, and an increasing fight to disseminate the scientific facts and raise our level of achievement can overcome . . . prejudice which to a large extent is founded on ignorance.

CHARLES DREW (1904—1950)

American scientist and educator

EDUCATION IS THE JEWEL CASTING BRILLIANCE INTO THE FUTURE.

MARIE EVANS (B. 1923)

American poet

Education is the only solid bridge you can rely on to transport you over your troubled waters. So, on that premise, I'll say to you: Use that bridge to get on the other side where you can stand up and be counted, thereby leaving your footsteps in the sand of time for others to follow.

CHRISTINE FORTE (B. 1906)

American writer

As the wound inflames the finger, so thought inflames the mind.
ETHIOPIAN PROVERB

Concerning our children's minds, there is no place for local option.
THURGOOD MARSHALL (1908—1993)
American Supreme Court Justice

INSTRUCTION IN YOUTH IS LIKE ENGRAVING IN STONE.
LIBYAN PROVERB

We're in an era when higher education is under attack from conservatives for what is thought to be a liberal bent.
RUTH J. SIMMONS (B. 1946)
American educator and president of Smith College

Black studies will be revolutionary or it will be useless if not detrimental.
NATHAN HARE (B. 1941)
American sociologist

NOT ONLY DO WE RECRUIT YOU, WE GRADUATE YOU.
MOTTO OF LANGSTON UNIVERSITY

I learned that along with the towering achievements of the cultures of ancient Greece and China there stood the culture of Africa.
PAUL ROBESON (1898—1976)
American actor and singer

THE FIRST THING WE ARE DOING IS TRYING TO GET INTO EVERY SCHOOL, PRIVATE, PUBLIC OR OTHERWISE, NEGRO LITERATURE AND HISTORY. WE ARE NOT TRYING TO DISPLACE ANY OTHER LITERATURE OR HISTORY, BUT TRYING TO GET ALL CHILDREN OF THE COUNTRY ACQUAINTED WITH THE NEGRO. . . . I THINK YOU WILL BE SURPRISED TO KNOW HOW MANY SCHOOLS, NORTH AND SOUTH, EVEN OUR OWN SCHOOLS WHERE OUR CHILDREN ARE TAUGHT NOTHING EXCEPT LITERATURE OF THE CAUCASIAN RACE. THE FIRST LAW OF NATURE IS SELF-PRESERVATION.

MARGARET JAMES [MURRAY] WASHINGTON (1856—1925)
American educator, suffragist, and civil rights activist

As a Black child, just attending school is almost an act of sedition. Education is considered "bad" for us . . . unnecessary.

MIRIAM MAKEBA (B. 1932)
South African singer

KNOWLEDGE IS THE PRIME NEED OF THE HOUR.

MARY McLEOD BETHUNE (1875—1955)
American educator, civil rights leader, and co-founder of Bethune-Cookman College

I made up my mind that I would die to see my people taught. I was willing to prepare to die from my people, for I could not rest till my people were educated.

KATE DRUMGOLD
American abolitionist

There must always be the continuing struggle to make the increasing knowledge of the world bear some fruit in increasing understanding and in the production of human happiness.

CHARLES DREW (1904—1950)
American scientist and educator

Excellence is not an act but a habit. The things you do most are the things you do best.

MARVA NETTLES COLLINS (B. 1936)
American educator

I LIVED IN LIBRARIES. I READ EVERYTHING. THAT'S WHY I SAY THERE'S NO EXCUSE FOR A PERSON TODAY NOT TO TAKE ADVANTAGE OF ALL THE OPPORTUNITIES THAT ARE AVAILABLE. THERE IS NO EXCUSE FOR IGNORANCE.

HAZEL B. GARLAND (1913—1988)
American journalist and editor

The lack of knowledge is darker than night.

AFRICAN PROVERB

We must remember that intelligence is not enough. Intelligence plus character—this is the goal of true education.

MARTIN LUTHER KING, JR. (1929—1968)
American cleric, civil rights leader, and writer

THERE IS NO LEARNING WITHOUT CONTROVERSY.

ANDREW YOUNG (B. 1932)

American cleric, politician, and civil rights activist

When you're through learning, you're through.

VERNON LAW

American civil rights activist

IGNORANCE DOESN'T KILL YOU, BUT IT MAKES YOU SWEAT A LOT.

HAITIAN PROVERB

Not to know is bad; not to wish to know is worse.

AFRICAN PROVERB

I'm educated because I went to school, because I was taught. You're educated because you went to school, were taught. I'm cultured because my people had the education and the means to achieve a good standard of living; that's the reason you're cultured. . . . Going to school and having money doesn't make me European. Having no schools and no money doesn't make the African primitive.

ESLANDA GOODE ROBESON (1896–1965)

American chemist, Pan-Africanist, anthropologist, and writer

IT TAKES A WHOLE VILLAGE TO EDUCATE A CHILD.

NIGERIAN PROVERB

Is it really so great a leap to teach our children that theft, excess, and bigotry are wrong, or that respecting the persons, property, and privacy of others is right?

STEPHEN L. CARTER (B. 1954)
American lawyer and writer

[I']ll be talking about saving lives. I'm gonna be talking about going back to school, being educated, putting people that go to school up instead of putting them down. It's a little bit of everything, all sorts of ingredients, sort of like a gumbo.

WILLIE D
American musician

COLLEGE AIN'T SO MUCH WHERE YOU BEEN AS HOW YOU TALK WHEN YOU COME BACK.

OSSIE DAVIS (B. 1917)
American actor, playwright, and director

View learning and skill building as a lifelong endeavor . . . and above all stay focused.

KAREN GRACE-BAKER
American executive

THE SPEAKERS IN THIS CHAPTER remind us that acceptance is the key to good family relations.

By accepting our family, we learn to accept others. And when the acceptance we offer to others is given to us in return, we see ourselves as something special. Our self-esteem is enhanced as others offer us guidance while also respecting our independence. Thus, we fashion ourselves into adults and bloom like flowers.

Respecting the wisdom and guidance of our elders, loving our children unconditionally, and creating a sense of everlasting unity among family occupies each speaker's attention in this chapter. Their voices speak of both the turbulence and the joy that every family experiences. They believe a strong nuclear family is the core of a stable community. The definition of what constitutes a family is flexible—a family can be found wherever there are people caring for and looking out for each other.

[F]AMILY IS VERY IMPORTANT TO MY EXISTENCE.

GREGORY HINES (B. 1946)
American dancer and actor

[M]y family directly and my people indirectly have given me a kind of strength that enables me to go anywhere.

MAYA ANGELOU (B. 1928)
American poet and writer

Acting is just a way of making a living. The family is life.

DENZEL WASHINGTON (B. 1954)
American actor

HOWEVER FAMOUS A MAN IS OUTSIDE, IF HE IS NOT RESPECTED INSIDE HIS OWN HOME, HE IS LIKE A BIRD WITH BEAUTIFUL FEATHERS, WONDERFUL ON THE OUTSIDE, BUT ORDINARY WITHIN.

CYPRIAN EKWENSI (B. 1921)
Nigerian writer

The dissolution of the family unit is more than just a minority problem. Every family needs the love and input from grandma, grandpa, and mom and dad—and those homeless kids need the attention, love, and consistency only a family can bring.

LOUIS GOSSET, JR. (B. 1936)

American actor

Everybody in the family survived. Nobody does drugs, nobody gets shot at. [I]t was because we were afraid of mama's voice. We didn't know how poor we were. We were rich as a family.

FLORENCE GRIFFITH JOYNER (B. 1959)

American athlete

MONEY AND CHILDREN DON'T GO TOGETHER: IF YOU SPENT ALL YOUR TIME MAKING MONEY AND GETTING RICH, THE GODS WOULDN'T GIVE YOU ANY CHILDREN, IF YOU WANTED CHILDREN YOU HAD TO FORGET MONEY AND BE CONTENT TO BE POOR.

BUCHI EMECHETA (B. 1944)

Nigerian writer

In Yoruba, we don't count our children. We just say gods have been kind to us.

WOLE SOYINKA (B. 1935)

Nigerian playwright

You may be a pain in the ass, and you may be bad, but child, you belong to me.

RAY CHARLES (B. 1930)
American musician

IN THE EYES OF ITS MOTHER, EVERY BEETLE IS A GAZELLE.
MOROCCAN PROVERB

May the saving grace of the mother-heart save humanity.

GEORGIA DOUGLAS JOHNSON (1886—1966)
American poet

Hit a child and quarrel with its mother.

NIGERIAN PROVERB

THE CALVES FOLLOW THEIR MOTHERS. THE YOUNG PLANT GROWS UP NEAR THE PARENT STEM. THE YOUNG ANTELOPE LEAPS WHERE ITS MOTHER HAS LEAPED.
ZULU PROVERB

The other day there was a guy driving me from Nashua College whose brother is gay and has AIDS, and won't tell his parents. And I said, "Look, tell your brother to tell your mom. Mothers will love you regardless."

ARTHUR ASHE (1943—1993)
American athlete

It wasn't like the minister said something bad about my mama. That would have caused a major problem between us. But as far as I know, the minister has never said anything bad about my mama.

CORNEL WEST (B. 1953)
American educator, scholar, and writer

WE WILL DIE WITHOUT OUR YOUNG PEOPLE.

ALEX HALEY (1921—1992)
American writer

Often when we have given to our child, we beg him to give us a little, not because we want to eat it but because we want to test the child. We want to know whether he is the kind of person who will give out or whether he will clutch everything to his chest when he grows up.

CHINUA ACHEBE (B. 1930)
Nigerian writer

MANY THINGS WE NEED CAN WAIT. THE CHILDREN CANNOT.

AGNES D. LATTIMER (B. 1928)
American physician

I'm the mother of the world. All these children are mine. Anybody let me love 'em, they're mine. Those that don't let me love 'em, then I love 'em anyhow.

WILLIE MAE FORD SMITH (B. 1904)
American singer

CHARITY BEGINS AT HOME AND THEN SPREADS AROUND.

MARY ANN PROUT (1810—1884)

American educator

Whether you have a Ph.D. or a D.D., or no D., we're in this to-gether. Whether you're from Morehouse or No House, we're in this bag together.

FANNIE LOU HAMER (1917—1977)

American civil rights leader

He is a fool who treats his brother worse than a stranger.

NIGERIAN PROVERB

THERE IS NO PROBLEM WE CAN'T SOLVE IF WE CAN CORRAL OUR RESOURCES BEHIND IT. THAT MEANS PEOPLE, THAT MEANS MONEY, THAT MEANS THE GOOD WILL AND COOPERATION OF A LARGE SEGMENT OF THE PEOPLE.

CORETTA SCOTT KING (B. 1927)

American civil rights activist

[I]t was proposed . . . that a society should be formed, without regard to religious tenets, provided, the persons lived an orderly and sober life, in order to support one another in sickness, and for the benefit of their widows and fatherless children.

THE FREE AFRICA SOCIETY (1787)

A BROTHER IS LIKE ONE'S SHOULDER.
SOMALIAN PROVERB

Our only care need be the intrinsic worth of our contributions.

ANNA JULIA COOPER (1859—1964)
American educator and social activist

A moral life is a life of activity in society.

E. FRANKLIN FRAZIER (1894—1962)
American sociologist and educator

YOU MUST GIVE OF YOURSELF IN ORDER TO BE WORTHY.
HATTIE BESSENT (B. 1926)
American administrator, researcher, educator, and writer

I'm not the kind of musician you hear saying "my music." I don't think I have music. I think everybody gets music from the community they come from.

HUGH MASEKELA (B. 1939)
American musician

I am grateful to all those people for the experiences that have taught me the joy of diversity, understanding, and tolerance.

VALERIE VAZ
American journalist

I always wanted to be somebody. If I made it, it's half because I was game enough to take a lot of punishment along the way, and half because there were a lot of people who cared enough to help me.

ALTHEA GIBSON DARBEN (B. 1927)
American athlete

ANCESTORS, ANCESTORS GUIDE ME TO WHATEVER I'M LOOKING FOR, WHATEVER IT MAY BE.
ETHIOPIAN PROVERB

Hard times are getting so much harder that it's forcing Black people to turn to one another. We had become so content and so "mind your business" till we found out that "mind your business" hasn't helped our survival as a community.

SISTER SOULJAH [LISA WILLIAMSON]
American musician and writer

WHEN YOU KILL THE ANCESTOR, YOU KILL YOURSELF.
TONI MORRISON (B. 1931)
American writer

I cannot allow myself to be insensitive to the wrongs and sufferings of any part of the great family of man.

FREDERICK DOUGLASS (C. 1817—1895)
American writer and abolitionist

My great-grandmama told my grandmama the part she lived through
that my grandmama didn't live through and my grandmama told my
mama what they both lived through and we were supposed to pass
it down like that from generation so we'd never forget.

GAYLE JONES (B. 1949)
American writer

**[A]T 26 I HAVE TAKEN THE BATON. MY MOTHER LIVED HER
LIFE, NOW I AM LIVING MINE. HER DEATH HAS PAVED THE WAY
FOR MY BIRTH. I AM BLOOMING, AND THAT IS ONLY A CAUSE FOR
CELEBRATION.**

IPELERY KGOSITSILE
American actress and writer

GENDER

THERE IS NO WAR BETWEEN the sexes in this chapter. Instead we are charged with the task of building unity among women and men. One speaker after another points out that division among black men and women leads to destruction. For that reason, there is a call for feminism to include the fight against racism in its agenda. And men are implored to see the beauty in themselves and to reflect it by treating women with honor and respect.

If there is a war between the sexes, you'll find a truce on these pages. These men and women are learning about themselves and one another. Here they celebrate their differences and look for common ground.

Their words are not always gentle, but in the end these speakers challenge assumptions, toss stereotypes aside, and leave us with compassion as the great equalizer. Regardless of their politics or sexual preferences they accept one another.

Let their words encourage you to touch people kindly, softly, with passion, and with pride.

THE TRUE WORTH OF A RACE MUST BE MEASURED BY THE CHARACTER OF ITS WOMANHOOD. . . .

MARY McLEOD BETHUNE (1875—1955)

American educator, civil rights activist, and co-founder of Bethune-Cookman College

I was about eight years old and I opened the door one day and there was Mary McLeod Bethune. I remember sitting on the floor playing as my mother and she talked. Mrs. Bethune was saying that colored women needed to stop playing bridge and start building bridges.

BISHOP LEOTINE T.C. KELLY (B. 1920)

American cleric

My girls and women, you should live that the world may be better by your having lived in it.

CLARA A. HOWARD (1866—1935)

American educator and missionary

The world cannot move without woman's sharing in the movement, and to help give a right impetus that movement is woman's highest privilege.

FRANCES E.W. HARPER (1825—1911)
American poet and writer

TO WOMAN HAS BEEN COMMITTED THE RESPONSIBILITY OF MAKING THE LAWS OF SOCIETY, MAKING ENVIRONMENTS FOR CHILDREN. SHE HAS THE PRIVILEGE AND AUTHORITY, GOD-GIVEN, TO HELP DEVELOP INTO A NOBLE MAN OR WOMAN THE YOUNG LIFE COMMITTED TO HER CARE. THERE IS NO NOBLER WORK ENTRUSTED TO THE HANDS OF MORTALS.

LUCY CRAFT LANEY (1854—1933)
American educator

Black women are nurturers. We nurture our families by seriously listening to and seriously considering what they tell us.

SAMELLA LEWIS
American artist, writer, and educator

We survive because of what I call the secret of Black women. We've always had to cope, and history and circumstance have only strengthened us.

BUCHI EMECHETA (B. 1944)
Nigerian writer

When people talk about the "strength" of Black women . . . they ignore the reality that to be strong in the face of oppression is not the same as overcoming oppression, that endurance is not to be confused with transformation.

BELL HOOKS (B. 1955)

American educator, writer, and social activist

We are all in a constant state of change—those changes are affected by personal experiences and expectations. Throughout my life, I fight to continue to say—"I am me," "I am black," "I am female"—that is all that's real.

COLLEEN MCELROY (B. 1935)

American educator

[A] GIRL HAS GOT TO BE A DAUGHTER FIRST. SHE HAS TO LEARN THAT. AND IF SHE NEVER LEARNS HOW TO BE A DAUGHTER, SHE CAN'T LEARN HOW TO BE A WOMAN.

TONI MORRISON (B. 1931)

American writer

It is rare that one can see in a little boy the promise of a man, but one can almost always see in a little girl the threat of a woman.

ALEXANDRE DUMAS (1824—1895)

French writer

WHATEVER I HAVE FACED AS A WOMAN IS PROBABLY A LOT MORE SUBTLE THAN WHAT I HAVE FACED AS A BLACK WOMAN.

CHARLAYNE HUNTER-GAULT (B. 1942)

American journalist

I am a woman and I write from that experience. I am a Black woman and I write from that experience. I do not feel inhibited or bound by what I am. That does not mean that I have never had bad scenes related to being Black and/or a woman; it means that other people's craziness has not managed to make me crazy.

LUCILLE CLIFTON (B. 1936)

American writer

The way in which I have often described this for myself, as a Black woman, is that (Black women's) literature helps me to know I'm not hallucinating. Because much of one's life from the point of view of a Black woman could be seen as a hallucination from what society tells you.

BARBARA CHRISTIAN (B. 1943)

American writer and educator

I like telling stories and controlling worlds. In my world, Black women can do anything. They ride horses and fly from trapezes; they are in the future as well as in the past.

JULIE DASH (B. 1952)

American filmmaker

I'M NOT A FEMINIST . . . I'M JUST A PROUD BLACK WOMAN.

QUEEN LATIFAH (B. 1970)
American actress and rap artist

[D]o you mean to say that you don't believe in working in the interest of women? That's what feminism is: It's working to assure that women are not limited in their options and opportunities by virtue of their gender.

FAYE WATTLETON (B. 1943)
American writer, women's rights activist, and former president of Planned Parenthood

When feminism does not explicitly oppose racism, and when anti-racism does not incorporate opposition to patriarchy, race, and gender, politics often end up being antagonistic to one another and both interests lose.

KIMBERLE CRENSHAW (B. 1959)
American writer

Only equals can be friends
ETHIOPIAN PROVERB

BLACK WOMEN PUT A HEAVIER EMPHASIS ON COLLECTIVITY. WE HAVEN'T BEEN TAUGHT THAT INDIVIDUAL GAIN IS MORE IMPORTANT THAN EVERYTHING ELSE.

PATRICIA REID-MERRITT
American educator and writer

By act of Congress, male officers are gentlemen, by act of God, we [female officers] are ladies. We don't have to be little mini-men and try to be masculine and use obscene language to come across. I can take you and flip you on the floor and put your arms behind your back and you'll never move again, without you ever knowing I can do it.

SHERIAN GRACE CADORIA (B. 1940)
American military general

A WOMAN IS A WOMAN UNTIL THE DAY SHE DIES, BUT A MAN'S A MAN ONLY AS LONG AS HE CAN.

JACKIE "MOMS" MABLEY (1894—1975)
American comedian and actress

For as unseemly as it may appear now-a-days for a woman to preach, it should be remembered that nothing is impossible with God. And why should it be thought impossible, heterodox, and improper, for woman to preach? Seeing the Savior died for woman as well as man. . . .

JARENA LEE (C. 1783–C. 1850)
American cleric

I'm a big believer in inner beauty. . . . To me, what makes a woman truly beautiful has little to do with the physical. It's a certain serenity; it's about being confident in yourself and centered in belief. It's about loving who you are and treating others as you want to be treated.

HALLE BERRY (B. 1969)
American actress

[N]o black woman can become an intellectual without de-colonizing her mind.

BELL HOOKS (B. 1955)
American educator, social activist, and writer

Say "Sister" next time!

GEORGIA E. PATTON WASHINGTON (1864—1900)
American physician

I am not afraid to trust my sisters—not I.

ANGELINA GRIMKE (1805—1879)
American abolitionist, suffragist, and writer

SISTERS HAVE TAUGHT ME THAT WE SHOULD LISTEN TO THE POETRY WITHIN, CAPTURE AND EXPRESS OUR INNER BEAUTY AS A PART OF OUR POLITICAL AND SOCIAL BEING.

MANNING MARABLE, PH.D. (B. 1948)
American historian

True chivalry respects all womanhood.

IDA B. WELLS (1862—1931)
American educator, civil rights leader, and journalist

One distressing thing is the way men react to women who assert their equality: their ultimate weapon is to call them un-feminine. They think she is anti-male; they even whisper that she is probably a lesbian.

SHIRLEY CHISHOLM (B. 1924)
American politician and first black congresswoman

A Black person in America, where he or she achieves a level of success and power and authority, faces in some cases a hostile environment . . . people are jealous; they don't like it; they resent it. They want to give all kinds of reasons why you are there, other than the reason that you are good and confident and smart.

RON BROWN (1941—1996)
American presidential cabinet member

Black is beautiful when it is a slum kid studying to enter college, when it is a man learning new skills for a new job. . . .

WHITNEY M. YOUNG, JR. (1921—1971)
American civil rights activist

EVERYTHING IN THIS SOCIETY IS GEARED TO KEEPING A BLACK BOY FROM GROWING TO MANHOOD, BUT HE HAS TO TRY FOR HIMSELF.

JOHN KILLENS (B. 1916)
American writer

[A]t each critical point of development, the Black boy is told to hold back, to constrict, to subvert, and to camouflage his normal masculinity.

WILLIAM H. GRIER, M.D.
American scientist and writer

We have to . . . teach Black boys social demand to add significance to the process of becoming a man.

NATHAN HARE (B. 1934)
American sociologist

YOUNG BLACK MEN ARE NEVER AFFORDED A CHILDHOOD OR IN-NOCENCE, OR THE BENEFIT OF DOUBT, BUT IN ALL OF IT, WE ARE GROWING. WE SEEK NOTHING LESS THAN FULL HUMANITY.

ROHAN B. PRESTON
American writer

You cannot do this to me. You cannot compel my definition. You cannot force me down. You cannot repress me. I will speak. I will speak out of who I am.

HOUSTON BAKER
American educator

I am here to demand my rights and to hurl thunderbolts at the man who would dare to cross the threshold of my manhood.

HENRY McNEAL TURNER (1833—1915)
American abolitionist and cleric

BEING A BLACK MAN IN AMERICA IS LIKE HAVING ANOTHER JOB.

ARTHUR ASHE (1943—1993)

American athlete and social activist

Treat us like men, and there is no danger, but we will all live in peace and happiness together.

DAVID WALKER (1785—1830)

American writer and abolitionist

OH, IT WAS HELL TO BE A MAN OF COLOR, INTELLECTUALLY AND NATURALLY HUMAN IN THE WHITE WORLD. EXCEPT FOR A SUPER-MAN, ALMOST IMPOSSIBLE.

CLAUDE MCKAY (1891—1948)

American poet

The blues are perhaps the clearest statement of the Black man's social attitude about love, sexuality, travel, work, and the general conditions of his life.

LEONARD GOINES

American educator

When you look at a fellow, if you have taught yourself to look for it, you can see his song written on him. It will tell you what kind of man he is in the world.

AUGUST WILSON (B. 1945)

American playwright

The Black man is the result of a multiplicity of experiences, some barely remembered, but all sensed in some mysterious manner when the loneliness is deep enough or the togetherness is strong enough.

DON EVAN (B. 1938)
American playwright and actor

I have been challenged in the past because people don't always understand me. I've always been my own man, my own person. I haven't done too much of anything that did not fit me. I've always tried to tailor situations to fit me.

DEXTER KING (B. 1962)
American politician [son of Martin Luther King, Jr.]

In the Black man's quest for liberation all activities of that quest should reflect an attempt to create a better world in which to live the liberation.

MELBA BOYD (B. 1950)
American educator

BLACK MEN LOVING BLACK MEN IS THE REVOLUTIONARY ACT.

MARLON RIGGS (1957—1994)
American filmmaker

We need a masculinity that brings us more into contact with one another. A masculinity that is more intimate and humane.

ESSEX HEMPHILL
American poet

I felt embraced by the heart of a million Black men whose unbridled power seemed to shake the earth beneath my feet. In a spiritual sense, I was home.

MICHAEL H. COTTMAN
American journalist

[A]S BLACK MEN, I, AND EVERYONE WHO LOOKS AT ME, LIVE IN AN EXTREME WORLD.

DARRELL DAWSEY
American writer

Writing has made me a better man. It has put me in contact with those fleeting moments which prove the existence.

ISHMAEL REED (B. 1938)
American writer

I'm both Black and gay. As far as I'm concerned, I've hit the jackpot.

JAMES BALDWIN (1924—1987)
American writer

I went through a whole lot when I was a boy. They called me sissy, punk, freak, and faggot. If I ever went out to friends' houses on my own, the guys would try to catch me, about eight or twenty of them together. They would run me. I never knew I could run so fast, but I was scared. They would jump on me, y'know, cause they didn't like my actions. . . .

"LITTLE" RICHARD PENNIMAN
American musician, singer, and composer

I think the gay community has a moral obligation . . . to do whatever is possible to encourage more and more gays to come out of the closet. God knows, people stay in the closet because it's very painful to come out.

BAYARD RUSTIN (1910—1987)
American civil rights activist

Homosexuality is not a crime. People have to realize that although you may be different, you must be treated in the same way as every other South African.

NELSON MANDELA (B. 1918)
president of South Africa

Some of most brilliant teachers and some of my classmates were gay. They were just part of the community of people I think that is what is important to understand.

JESSE JACKSON (B.1941)
American cleric and civil rights leader

HOMOPHOBIA DIVIDES BLACK PEOPLE AS POLITICAL ALLIES, IT CUTS OFF POLITICAL GROWTH, STIFLES REVOLUTION, AND PERPETUATES PATRIARCHAL DOMINATION.

CHERYL CLARK (B. 1947)
American writer

HOMOSEXUALITY IS A SICKNESS, JUST [LIKE] BABY-RAPE OR WANTING TO BECOME HEAD OF GENERAL MOTORS.

ELDRIDGE CLEAVER (B. 1935)

American social activist and writer

We must change homosexual behavior and get rid of the circumstances that bring it about.

LOUIS FARRAKHAN (B. 1933)

American cleric [head of the Nation of Islam]

I BELIEVE IN AN AMERICA THAT DOES NOT DISCRIMINATE BECAUSE OF SEXUAL ORIENTATION.

DAVID DINKINS (B. 1927)

American politician and educator

And maybe I'm now injecting some of my own prejudice by saying that "even a homosexual can be a revolutionary." Quite on the contrary, maybe a homosexual could be the most revolutionary.

HUEY NEWTON (1944—1994)

American political activist and co-founder of the Black Panther Party

Someday I expect the "discrete" lesbian will not turn her head on the streets at the sight of the "butch" strolling hand in hand with her friend in their trousers and definitive haircuts. But for the moment it still disturbs.

LORRAINE HANSBERRY (1930—1965)

American playwright

Went out last night with a crowd of my friends. They must've been women, 'cause I don't like men.

GERTRUDE "MA" RAINEY (1886—1939)
American singer

By being sexually independent of men, lesbian, by their very existence, call into question society's definition of woman at its deepest level.

BARBARA CHRISTIAN (B. 1943)
American educator and writer

[S]OME PROFESSIONS SHOULDN'T BE OPEN TO WOMEN BECAUSE THEY CAN'T HANDLE CERTAIN JOBS, LIKE CONSTRUCTION WORK. LESBIAN, MAYBE, BUT NOT WOMEN.

MUHAMMAD ALI [CASSIUS CLAY] (B. 1942)
American athlete

Sex and racism have always been tied together. Look at the thousands of Black men who got lynched and castrated. The reason the Klan came into being was to protect white Southern women.

SHELTON "SPIKE" LEE
American filmmaker

[L]YNCHING WAS . . . A WOMAN'S ISSUE: IT HAD AS MUCH TO DO WITH IDEAS OF GENDER AS IT HAD WITH RACE.

PAULA GIDDINGS (B. 1948)
American writer and educator

WHEN YOU ARE ANCHORED, YOU DON'T FEAR ANYTHING AND YOU REALLY DO BELIEVE THERE AIN'T NO MOUNTAIN HIGH ENOUGH.

VERNON JORDAN (B. 1935)

American lawyer

There is no person who is not a member of a race, a group, a family of humankind. Nobody exists alone. We are each a part of a specific collective past. . . .

EUGENIA COLLIER (B. 1928)

American writer

GROWTH

CELEBRATE THE CHANGES IN YOUR life that can lead to your growth. Acknowledge how frightening change can be and embrace those changes. This message isn't necessarily a religious one but it does have a spiritual basis. It's founded on the belief that change is inevitable. It will come no matter what. Change is how the universe was formed.

As elements of the universe, we grow when we allow ourselves to change. The wisest person is the one who is receptive to the changes that make spiritual growth possible.

The speakers here remind us not to confuse maturity with aging. You don't necessarily become wise with age. It's spiritual, intellectual, and emotional growth that leads to wisdom. Getting taller doesn't signal change, nor do a few gray hairs. Growth and change are significant when they occur invisibly, deep inside a person's heart.

IF YOU UNDERSTAND THE BEGINNING WELL, THE END WILL NOT TROUBLE YOU.

ASHANTI PROVERB

For me, life is all about growth.

JANET JACKSON (B. 1966)
American singer

An athlete retires twice. The first time is when they don't renew your contract. But for a couple of years afterwards you will think you could get in shape again and play another season or two. Then one day you look in the mirror and the reality finally sinks in that it's time to find something else to do with the rest of your life.

ARTHUR ASHE (1943–1993)
American athlete

I'M USING MOST OF WHAT I'VE LEARNED IN MY FIRST FIFTY YEARS AND APPLYING IT.

HARVEY CLARK (B. 1947)
American broadcast journalist

like my life better each year. I have a bigger base of knowledge to draw on.

A. BRUCE CRAWLEY (B. 1946)
American executive

IT'S BETTER TO LOOK AHEAD AND PREPARE THAN TO LOOK BACK AND REGRET.

JACKIE JOYNER-KERSEE (B. 1962)
American athlete

People won't forget, but they're going to say, "Great. After his downfall, the guy took care of his problems and won again." That will be the biggest thrill of my life.

BEN JOHNSON (B. 1961)
Canadian athlete

I AM TRAVELING ON A SPIRITUAL MISSION, BUT SOMETIMES I GET DISTRACTED.

JULIE DASH (B. T.K)
American filmmaker

f you can find someone you can really talk to, it can help you grow in many ways.

STEPHANIE MILLS (B. 1957)
American actress and singer

[F]riends have been so important to my growth and survival.

THULANI DAVIS
American writer

The people with whom we have contact are the chisels and hammers that craft what we will become. Our life's journey is an ever-unfolding work of art that tells the story of where we have been and with whom we have traveled.

IYANLA VANZANT
American-born Yoruba priestess and writer

LET ME BE THE LEAF JUST LAYING AT THE FOOT OF THE TREE, GIVING IT SUBSTANCE TO GROW.

WILLIE MAE FORD SMITH (B. 1904)
American singer

MY SOUL HAS GROWN DEEP LIKE THE RIVERS.

LANGSTON HUGHES (1902–1967)
American poet and writer

I have reached a point in my life where I understand the pain and the challenges, and my attitude is one of standing with open arms to meet all of them.

MYRLIE EVERS (B. 1933)
American civil rights activist, former head of NAACP[widow of Medgar Evers]

There are roads out of the secret places within us along which we all must move as we go to touch others.

ROMARE BEARDEN (1914–1988)
American artist

All my growth and development led me to believe that if you really do the right thing, and if you play by the rules, and if you've got good enough, solid judgment and common sense, that you're going to be able to do whatever you want to do with your life.

BARBARA JORDAN (B. 1936)
American politician

I NEVER WANTED TO SIT IN THIS CHAIR UNTIL I FELT IN MY MIND AND HEART THAT I HAD THE NECESSARY EXPERIENCE TO ANCHOR.

BERNARD SHAW (B. 1940)
American journalist

As they become known and accepted to ourselves, our feelings, and the honest exploration of them, become sanctuaries and fortresses and spawning grounds for the most radical and daring of ideas, the house of difference so necessary to change and the conceptualization of any meaningful action.

AUDRE LORDE (1934–1992)
American poet and writer

RATHER THAN FACE HOW BAD I TRULY FELT . . . I STUFFED MYSELF WITH STUFF, PUFFED MYSELF UP WITH A FALSE SENSE OF POWER AND IMPORTANCE.

PATTI AUSTIN (B. 1948)
American singer

It is his life and no mere abstraction in someone's head. He must live it and try consciously to grasp its complexity until he can change it; [and] he must live as he changes it.

RALPH ELLISON (1914–1994)
American writer

SINCE WE LIVE IN A CHANGING UNIVERSE, WHY DO MEN OPPOSE CHANGE? IF A ROCK IS IN THE WAY, THE ROOT OF A TREE WILL CHANGE ITS DIRECTION. THE DUMBEST ANIMALS TRY TO ADAPT THEMSELVES TO CHANGED CONDITIONS. EVEN A RAT WILL CHANGE ITS TACTICS TO GET A PIECE OF CHEESE.

MELVIN TOLSON (1900–1966)
American poet and educator

It occurs to me that much organizational grief could be avoided if people understood that partnership in misery does not necessarily provide for partnership for change.

JUNE JORDAN (B. 1936)
American poet and social activist

As you open up and out to the world, as you grow in awareness and empathy for human beings in nations near and far, you may see more acutely, or perhaps anew, the condition of those in your own backyard. This revelation, no matter how great or small, should not be an end in itself. It should . . . serve as a catalyst to your becoming an agent of change. It should bring to your remembrance the second part of the slogan from the Women's Conference in Nairobi: the imperative to "act locally."

FRANCES BEAL (1895–1953)
American social activist

[V]ictory is often a thing deferred, and rarely at the summit of courage. . . . What is at the summit of courage, I think is freedom. The freedom that comes with the knowledge that no earthly power can break you; that an unbroken spirit is the only thing you can live without; that in the end it is courage of conviction that moves things, that makes all changes possible.

PAULA GIDDINGS (B. T.K)
American educator and writer

[G]IVING PEOPLE CHOICES ENHANCES OUR CAPACITY TO ATTAIN DIGNITY AND REACH OUR CAPACITY AS PRODUCTIVE HUMAN BEINGS.
FAYE WATTLETON (B. 1943)
American women's rights activist and former president of Planned Parenthood

IDENTITY

THE TREE THAT BLOOMS IN THE open forest is visible and strong, but below the surface of the earth are the roots that give the tree it's true might. People get their strength from solid roots, too.

Locked inside each of us is the memory of our descendants, and those memories play a crucial role in helping us define our identities.

When the speakers in this chapter look at themselves, they see their own faces and the faces of our ancestors who came before them. Those ancestors were pioneers who opened doors for others to step through. It's their legacy that helped define how these speakers see themselves.

Whether discussing their private lives or their public accomplishments, the speakers regard everything in their lives as part of a rich tradition that stretches back through time. Within these pages, we're reminded that nothing we do as individuals is done in a vacuum—our actions reverberate across time and space. With that idea in mind, personal identity is a reflection of our community, the past, and the world. Our membership in society gives shape and depth to our individual identities.

BE BLACK, SHINE, AIM HIGH.

LEONTYNE PRICE (B. 1929)

American singer

Black is beautiful.

MARCUS GARVEY (1887–1940)

Jamaican social activist

MY BLACKNESS, TENDER AND STRONG, WOUNDED AND WISE. MY BLACKNESS IS THE BEAUTY OF THE LAND.

LANCE JEFFERS (B. 1919)

American poet

Beauty is here because I'm here.

17TH CENTURY AFRICAN-BORN DUTCH WOMAN

There is nothing so indigenous, so completely "made in America" as we Blacks.

WILLIAM WELLS-BROWN (1815–1884)

American writer

WE "OURSELVES" ARE HIGH ART.

NTOZAKE SHANGE (B. 1948)

American poet, playwright, and writer

I am not a ward of America; I am one of the first Americans to arrive on these shores.

JAMES BALDWIN (1924–1987)

American writer

THE BLACK CULTURAL TRADITION IN AMERICA IS A PRICELESS ONE, SPRINGING FROM THE CONFLUENCE OF GREAT MOTHER AFRICA AND THE ANGLO-SAXON, WESTERN EUROPEAN OVERFLOW. WE, AS BLACKS IN AMERICA, STILL DON'T REALIZE THIS, THAT WE ARE THE CITIZEN OF THE WORLD, AND AS SUCH SHOULD NEVER HAVE TO PLAY THE ROLE OF THE PROVERBIAL CRABS IN A BARREL.

CLIFORD MASON (B. 1932)

American educator and drama critic

Wherever we went, we found that people had been misled into believing that fifteen million American Negroes lived behind barbed wire. They were amazed that I had a law degree, attended a White church, and had never been to a segregated school.

EDITH S. SAMPSON (1901–1979)
American lawyer and judge

BLACK NEVER HAS BEEN THE COLOR OF SKIN . . . BUT A CULTURE.

JEAN CHILDS YOUNG (1933–1994)
American social activist and educator

A man without culture is like a grasshopper without wings.
AFRICAN PROVERB

We do not choose our cultures, we belong to them.
AIME CESAIRE (B. 1913)
Martiniquen writer

[O]ne of the bounties of Black culture is our ability to hear; if we were to throw this away in search of less (just language) we'd be damning ourselves.
NTOZAKE SHANGE (B. 1948)
American playwright and poet

IF YOU BLACK, YOU BLACK.

TED POSTON (1906–1974)
American journalist

Because just one drop of Black blood makes a colored man. One drop—you are a Negro! . . . Black is powerful.

LANGSTON HUGHES (1902–1967)

American poet and writer

I AM A LIVING SYMBOL OF THE WHITE MAN'S FEAR.

WINNIE MANDELA (B. 1934)

South African social activist

The African race is a rubber ball; the harder you dash it to the ground, the higher it will rise.

AFRICAN PROVERB

It never occurred to me that I was less than anybody else, because I was always ahead of everybody else.

OPRAH WINFREY (B. 1954)

American broadcaster and actress

WE ARE . . . A NATION OF DANCERS, SINGERS AND POETS.

OLAUDAN EQUIANO (C. 1745–1797)

African slave, writer, and abolitionist

I've got to go up there [stage] as an individual first, a Negro second. I've got to be a colored funny man, not a funny colored man.

DICK GREGORY (B. 1932)

American comedian, social activist, and writer

IF YOU GO INSIDE WHERE ALL PEOPLE ARE AND WHERE THE ESSENCE OF THEIR BEING IS, YOU ARE NOT GOING TO FIND ANYTHING TO HANG YOUR PREJUDICES ON.

BEAH RICHARDS (B. 1926)

American actress and poet

God is just. He deposits just as much genius in housing projects as he does in the suburbs. Just as many lawyers and legislators and the state directors can and have been in sharecroppers' shacks as in penthouses and high-income neighborhoods.

MICHAEL THURMOND

American administrator

IT'S NOT SO MUCH ABOUT WHERE YOU LIVE, IT'S WHAT'S LIVING IN YOU.

KWESI MFUME

American politician, social activist, and president of NAACP

I knew then who I was. I was a Negro, a human being with an invisible pigmentation which marked me a person to be hunted, hanged, abused, discriminated against, kept in poverty and ignorance, in order that those whose skin was white would have readily at hand a proof of their superiority, a proof patent and inclusive, accessible to the moron and the idiot as well as to the wise man and the genius.

WALTER WHITE (1893-1955)

American civil rights leader

[H]omeless in the land of our birth and worse off than strangers in the home of our nativity.

FRANCES E. W. HARPER (1825–1911)
American writer and poet

Yes, I admit a grievance
I also boldly challenge you—
Come stand where I once stood and fell!
I dare say you will do as well.

RAYMOND GARFIELD DANDRIDGE (1882–1930)
American writer

I WAS BORN POOR, I LIVED POOR, AND I'M GOING TO DIE POOR.
BILLIE HOLIDAY (1915–1959)
American singer

I was not born with a silver spoon in my mouth but instead, with a clothes basket upon my head.

MAGGIE LENA WALKER (1867–1934)
American financier, and philanthropist

[O]UT OF ONE MOUTH YOU'RE TOLD TO BE UNIVERSAL, AND OUT OF THE OTHER MOUTH YOU'RE TOLD YOU'RE NOT BLACK ENOUGH.
NAOMI LONG MADGETT (B. 1923)
American poet and publisher

I've been here 350 years but you've never seen me.

JAMES BALDWIN (1924–1987)

American writer

I CAME BACK TO MY NATIVE COUNTRY AND I COULDN'T RIDE IN THE FRONT OF THE BUS. I HAD TO GO TO THE BACK DOOR, I COULDN'T LIVE WHERE I WANTED. . . . I WASN'T INVITED UP TO SHAKE HANDS WITH HITLER, BUT I WASN'T INVITED TO THE WHITE HOUSE TO SHAKE HANDS WITH THE PRESIDENT, EITHER.

JESSE OWENS (1914–1980)

American athlete

You're only white as long as you think I'm black.

JAMES BALDWIN (1924–1987)

American writer

LOOK AT ME. NEVER MIND MY COLOR. JUST LOOK AT ME!

DIANA SANDS (1934–1973)

American singer

When people like me, they tell me it is in spite of my race. When they dislike me, they point out that it is not because of my colour. Either way, I am locked into the infernal circle.

FRANTZ FANON (1925–1961)

Martinique-born Algerian psychiatrist and writer

**IN THIS COUNTRY, AMERICAN MEANS WHITE. EVERYBODY ELSE
HAS TO HYPHENATE.**

TONI MORRISON (B. 1931)

American writer

It's hard being Black. You ever been Black? I was Black once—when
I was poor.

LARRY HOLMES (B. 1949)

American athlete

**MY FIGHT IS NOT TO BE A WHITE MAN IN A BLACK SKIN, BUT TO
INJECT SOME BLACK BLOOD, SOME BLACK INTELLIGENCE INTO THE
PALLID MAINSTREAM OF AMERICAN LIFE, CULTURALLY, SOCIALLY,
PSYCHOLOGICALLY, PHILOSOPHICALLY.**

JOHN OLIVER KILLENS (B. 1916)

American writer and educator

[I]n a way I'm working for the extinction of the African type in America because I want people to have their own businesses and hold high
political offices, but I know that when they do, they are going to become more and more a part of the American character. And the Black
soul is going to die in the middle of the White soul.

RUBYE DORIS ROBINSON (1942–1967)

American civil rights activist

YOU HAVE TO KNOW THAT YOUR REAL HOME IS WITHIN.

QUINCY JONES (B. 1933)

American entrepreneur, producer, and composer

I am of the African race, and in the color which is natural to them of the deepest dye, and it is under a sense of the most profound gratitude to the Supreme Ruler.

BENJAMIN BANNEKER (1731–1806)

American mathematician, astronomer, and social activist

Don't let your color fade into white. Don't let yourself be erased.

BRAZILIAN PROVERB

THE HOLE IN THE POOR MAN'S GARMENT IS SOON FILLED WITH THE PATCHWORK OF PRIDE. . . .

WOLE SOYINKA (B. 1935)

Nigerian writer

The best blood in my veins is African blood, and I am not ashamed of it.

FRANCES E. W. HARPER (1825–1911)

American poet, and writer

Once you know who you are, you don't have to worry anymore.

NIKKI GIOVANNI (B. 1943)

American poet, writer, and educator

Some people are your relatives but others are your ancestors, and you choose the ones you want to have as ancestors. You create yourself out of those values.

RALPH ELLISON (1914–1994)
American writer

YOU HAVE TO MAKE A DECISION ABOUT WHERE YOU'RE GOING TO GO WHETHER YOU ARE GOING TO ASSIMILATE OR SEPARATE.
AUGUST WILSON (B. 1945)
American playwright

When you're a Black child who believes she has no control over her life, you create your own definition of freedom.

MARITA GOLDEN
American writer

YOU NEVER FIND YOURSELF UNTIL YOU FACE THE TRUTH.
PEARL BAILEY (1918–1990)
American singer

Two things everybody's got tuh do for theyselves. They got tuh go tuh God, and they got tuh find out about livin' for theyselves.

ZORA NEALE HURSTON (1891–1960)
American writer and anthropologist

No matter how beautiful the idol, it must rest on a solid base.
LUBA PROVERB

[T]he most wonderful thing in the world is to be who you are.
LEONTYNE PRICE (B. 1928)
American singer

WHEN I DISCOVER WHO I AM, I'LL BE FREE.
RALPH ELLISON (1914–1994)
American writer

I constantly felt . . . a thumping from within unanswered by any beckoning from without.
ANNA JULIA COOPER (1859–1964)
American educator

MY MOTHER WAS A NEGRO AND I AM NOT ASHAMED TO CONFESS THAT MY PERSON MAKES OPEN DECLARATION OF MY LINEAGE. . . .
ALEXANDRE DUMAS (1824–1895)
French writer

I'd rather be Black than gay because when you're Black you don't have to tell your mother.
CHARLES PIERCE
American female impersonator

When I was a kid, Blacks would say, "Oh, we have some Irish in us and some Portuguese. We have better quality hair. We're better than other Blacks." I thought it was a load of bull. I have always considered myself a black man. What my mother has on her side is irrelevant. When I go for a role that was written for a White, it means nothing.

GREGORY HINES (B. 1946)

American dancer and actor

I've never forgotten where I come from—that's important to me.

REGGIE McFADDEN

American musician

I NOW WALK UPRIGHT IN THE WORLD, AND WHERE MY BODY GOES SO GOES MY SOUL.

ALVIN AUBERT (B. 1930)

American educator and writer

I cannot be bought and I will not be sold.

MARY MODJESKA MONTEITH SIMKINS (1899–1992)

American women's rights activist

SAY IT LOUD: I'M BLACK AND I'M PROUD.

JAMES BROWN (B. 1933)

American entertainer

INTIMACY

WHAT WORDS CAN DO JUSTICE TO the feeling of being in love? What grammatical construction can accurately reflect the experience of two bodies swept up in ardor and emotion?

Despite this struggle with language, we witness in these pages a torrent of passion and emotion made tangible by the power of words.

Do the speakers understand that their words might be held against them? That the messages here might be used to promote an ugly stereotype: That the erotic is wicked and fit only for a savage people? The answer is yes—they know. And thankfully they don't care. They speak boldly and openly of a sensual force that is at the core of every human being, creating new life and nurturing that life from one generation to the next.

Every page of this chapter expresses this force with sensitivity and emotion in a manner similar to a song. The song tells us that true intimacy is a product of love—a feeling for which there should never be shame.

TO LOVE IS TO MAKE ONE'S HEART A SWINGING DOOR.

HOWARD THURMAN (1899–1981)

American theologian, educator, and writer

Unconditional love not only means I am with you, but also I am for you, all the way, right or wrong. . . . Love is indescribable and unconditional. I could tell you a thousand things that it is not, but not one that is. Either you have it or you haven't, there's no proof of it.

EDWARD KENNEDY "DUKE" ELLINGTON (1899–1974)

American composer, musician, bandleader

LET YOUR LOVE BE LIKE THE MISTY RAINS, COMING SOFTLY, BUT FLOODING THE RIVER.

MADAGASCAR PROVERB

Without real love there's no music, no songs, no stories worth singing about.

KENNETH "BABYFACE" EDMONDS

American singer, composer, and producer

Everybody's the same when it comes to love. . . . When someone in the ghetto falls in love she hears bells—the same bells someone uptown hears when she falls in love.

BERRY GORDY, JR. (B. 1929)

American entrepreneur and founder of Motown Records

TALKING WITH ONE ANOTHER IS LOVING ONE ANOTHER.
KENYAN PROVERB

The capacity to love is so tied to being . . . able to move out of yourself and be with someone in a manner that is not about your desire to possess them, but to be with them, to be in union and communion.

BELL HOOKS (B. 1955)

American scholar, educator, social activist, and writer

LOVE IS LIKE A BABY; IT NEEDS TO BE TREATED GENTLY.
CONGOLESE PROVERB

All you need in the world is love and laughter. That's all anybody needs. To have love in one hand and laughter in the other.

AUGUST WILSON (B. 1945)

American playwright

[L]IFE IS LOVE—IF YOU DON'T LOVE, YOU DON'T MAKE IT.
ELLA MILLER (B. 1881)

American elder

When one is in love, a cliff becomes a meadow.
ETHIOPIAN PROVERB

ON THE WAY TO ONE'S BELOVED, THERE ARE NO HILLS.
KENYAN PROVERB

I have spread no snares today
I am caught in my love of you.
EGYPTIAN PROVERB

LOVE—THAT ARBITRARY AND INEXORABLE TYRANT.
HARRIET WILSON (1808–1870)
American abolitionist and writer

To experience the passion of hatred is to know the force of love.
ALFRED PASTER (B. 1947)
American writer

INTENSE LOVE IS OFTEN AKIN TO INTENSE SUFFERING.
FRANCES E. W. HARPER (1825–1911)
American poet and writer

If you love 'em in the morning with their eyes full of crust; if you love 'em at night with their hair full of rollers, chances are, you're in love.
MILES DAVIS (1926–1991)
American musician and composer

Everybody say "Love!"
RUPAUL (B. 1963)
American entertainer

LOVE IS LIKE PLAYING CHECKERS. YOU HAVE TO KNOW WHICH MAN TO MOVE.
JACKIE "MOMS" MABLEY (1894–1975)
American comedian and actress

The hen knows when it is daybreak, but allows the rooster to make the announcement.
ASHANTI PROVERB

[T]HERE ARE ANY NUMBER OF WOMEN AROUND WILLING TO WALK TEN PACES BACK TO GIVE HIM THE ILLUSION OF WALKING TEN PLACES AHEAD.
TONI CADE BAMBARA (1939–1985)
American writer

It is fallacious reasoning that in order for the Black man to be strong, the Black woman has to be weak.
FRANCIS BEALE (1898–1953)
American political activist

Woman without man is like a field without seed.
ETHIOPIAN PROVERB

The Black woman is both a ship and a safe harbor.

TONI MORRISON (B. 1931)

American writer

TO NO MODERN RACE DO ITS WOMEN MEAN SO MUCH AS TO THE NEGRO, NOR COME SO NEAR TO THE FULFILLMENT OF ITS MEANING.

W. E. B. DU BOIS (1868–1967)

American writer, educator, and social reformer

When the heart overflows, it comes out through the mouth.

CONGO PROVERB

I USED TO BE VERY COLD. WHEN YOU ARE COLD YOU MISS PASSION IN YOUR LIFE. I WENT FOR YEARS JUST LIKE ICE. I WAS KILLING MYSELF. I WAS NOT LOVING BACK.

LENA HORNE (B. 1917)

American entertainer

The heart of a man is a gift of God. Beware of neglecting it.

EGYPTIAN PROVERB

Happiness is perfume: you can't pour it on somebody else without getting a few drops on yourself.

JAMES VAN DER ZEE (1886–1983)

American photographer

[I]t is not the color of the skin that makes the man or the woman, but the principle formed in the soul.

MARIA W. STEWART (1803–1879)

American abolitionist and educator

I'VE ALWAYS FELT THAT COMPLEMENT OF OPPOSITES: BODY AND SOUL, SOLITUDE AND COMPANIONSHIP. . . .

JUDITH JAMISON (B. 1943)

American dancer and choreographer

The sexual and sensual impulses stir deep in the alluvium of the soul that animates us, its current eddying and surging like the inscrutable tides that stir the vast torrent of existence. All hail the delicious surges of lust that move our being.

DENNIS BRUTUS

Zimbabwean poet and educator

Our boasted civilization is but a veneer which cranks and scrubs off at the first impact of primal passions.

CHARLES W. CHESNUTT (1858–1932)

American writer

PASSIONS ARE DANGEROUS. THEY CAUSE YOU TO LUST AFTER OTHER MEN'S WIVES.

MARVIN GAYE (1939–1984)

American musician, singer, and composer

We tend to think of the erotic as an easy, tantalizing sexual arousal. I speak of the erotic as the deepest life force, a force which moves us toward living in a fundamental way.

AUDRE LORDE (1934–1992)

American poet and writer

To be sensual . . . is to respect and rejoice in the face of life, of life itself, and to be present in all that one does, from the effort of living to the breaking of bread.

JAMES BALDWIN (1924–1987)

American writer

The body of someone we love is not altogether naked, but is clothed and framed in our feelings.

ANATOLE BOYARD (1920–19TK)

American literary critic

ANYONE CAN HAVE SEX, BUT NOT EVERYONE CAN BE ROMANTIC.

TYRA BANKS (1973)

American model

TO UNDERSTAND HOW A SOCIETY FUNCTIONS, YOU MUST UNDERSTAND THE RELATIONSHIP BETWEEN THE MEN AND THE WOMEN.

ANGELA Y. DAVIS (B. 1944)

American political activist, educator, and writer

The man-woman thing is a dead subject. It's essentially a dead end. It's going to come down to one of two things: Either you're going to take off your clothes or not.

NIKKI GIOVANNI (B. 1943)

American poet, educator, and writer

Where sex talk is concerned, we all know folks who blanche at the mention of words like dick and pussy in polite discourse, but who relish putting their lips on the very genitalia those terms describe.

GREG TATE

American writer

If you want to lick the old woman's pot, scratch her back.

JAMAICAN PROVERB

A WOMAN'S LOVE IS A [MAN'S] PRIVILEGE AND NOT HIS RIGHT.

TERRY McMILLAN (B. 1951)

American writer

LET THEM WAIT. AND WAIT THEY DO!

JACKEE [JACKEE HARRY] (B. 1957)

American actress

I love Black women because a Black woman brought me into the world.

L. L. COOL J. [JAMES TODD SMITH] (1968)

American rap artist and actor

When I see a Black woman who is truly aware of who she is, I know I am looking at heaven walking on earth.

WESLEY SNIPES (B. 1962)
American actor

THE MORE BLACKNESS A WOMAN HAS, THE MORE BEAUTIFUL SHE IS.
ALEX HALEY (1921–1992)
American journalist and writer

I have dated women of other cultures, but I have a love for African-American women [because of] their strength and spirit.

STEVIE WONDER (B. 1950)
American singer, musician, and composer

THE BLACKER THE BERRY, THE SWEETER THE JUICE.
AFRICAN-AMERICAN PROVERB

My first husband looked like the sun. I used to say his name over and over again till it hung from my ears like diamonds.

SONIA SANCHEZ (B. 1935)
American writer, poet, and educator

[A] man has a special kind of relationship with a woman who has borne him children, which is itself the supreme demonstration [of love].

ES'KIA MPHAHLELE (B. 1919)
Pretorian writer

[M]y marriage is beautiful. Every day I discover that co-nurturing beats one partner doing it alone, that supporting a high-profile woman beats competing with her. And having confidence in our relationship is more satisfying than jealousy.

ARTHUR J. ROBINSON, JR.
American public-health service administrator [spouse of Johnetta Cole]

There is no secret to a long marriage—it's hard work. . . . It's serious business, and certainly not for cowards.

OSSIE DAVIS (B. 1917)
American actor, playwright, director, and social activist

MARRIAGE IS A PROCESS, WE'VE DISCOVERED. THE WEDDING IS THE EVENT. IT TAKES A LONG TIME TO REALLY BE MARRIED. ONE MARRIES MANY TIMES AT MANY LEVELS WITHIN A MARRIAGE. IF YOU HAVE MORE MARRIAGES THAN YOU HAVE DIVORCES WITHIN THE MARRIAGE, YOU'RE LUCKY AND YOU STICK IT OUT.

RUBY DEE (B. 1927)
American actress and social activist

Even the deepest love doesn't stop a marriage from being a constant struggle for control.

BILL COSBY (B. 1937)
American entertainer and writer

I BELIEVE IN THE INSTITUTION OF MARRIAGE, AND I INTEND TO KEEP TRYING TILL I GET IT RIGHT.

RICHARD PRYOR (B. 1940)

American comedian and actor

Men marry to make an end; women to make a beginning.

ALEXANDRE DUMAS (1824–1895)

French playwright

But if something happens and two people get along, the separation is nothing because it gives you that space, and you look forward to being together . . . all over again.

TINA TURNER (B. 1941)

American singer

HEARTS DO NOT MEET ONE ANOTHER LIKE ROADS.

IVORY COAST PROVERB

He didn't belong to me. He was the people's man. I never had the dream of falling head over heels with Prince Charming. There was no time for that.

WINNIE MANDELA (B. 1934)

South African social activist

A WOMAN WHO KNOWS HOW TO COOK IS MIGHTY PRETTY.

JAMAICAN PROVERB

I ain't good looking, but I'm somebody's angel child.

BESSIE SMITH (1894–1937)

American singer

YOU'VE GOT TO HAVE SOMETHING TO EAT AND A LITTLE LOVE IN YOUR LIFE BEFORE YOU CAN HOLD STILL FOR ANY DAMNED BODY'S SERMON ON HOW TO BEHAVE.

BILLIE HOLIDAY [ELEANOR FAGAN] (1915–1959)

American singer

I want everybody to practice safe sex, and that means using condoms. I want everybody to be aware of what is going on. . . .

EARVIN "MAGIC" JOHNSON (B. 1960)

American athlete

MOST PLAIN GIRLS ARE VIRTUOUS BECAUSE THE SCARCITY OF OPPORTUNITY TO DO OTHERWISE.

MAYA ANGELOU (B. 1928)

American poet and writer

If I could be the "condom queen" and get every young person who engaged in sex to use a condom in the United States, I would wear a crown on my head with a condom on it! I would!

JOCELYN ELDERS (B. 1933)

American physician, educator, and former Surgeon General

LIFE LESSONS

THE WISDOM OF AGE ISN'T LIMITED to people of advanced years.

Even children have learned a few things about life during their brief time on the planet. Young or old, rich or poor, life for us all is a road filled with landmarks, signs, twists, and turns.

So the insights that appear on the following pages speak to the most fundamental of human experiences—the experience of living. It's the one thing that we each share in common, a subject we all know well. The speakers here share with us what they've discovered on their own journeys. And in the manner of guides, they direct our attention to those places where the interests of all people meet—those hard-to-find places don't appear on maps other than the ones we all carry in our hearts.

BELIEVE IN LIFE!

W. E. B. DU BOIS (1868–1967)
American writer, educator, and social reformer

Always live each day as it comes.

GLORIA KNIGHT
Jamaican businesswoman

[LIFE] IS UPS AND DOWNS, IT'S 360 DEGREES. IT'S A CYCLE THAT ALWAYS CONTINUES.

GRAND PUBA [MAXWELL DIXON]
American rap artist

Humor is what you wish in your secret heart were not funny, but it is, and you must laugh. Humor is your unconscious therapy.

LANGSTON HUGHES (1902–1967)
American poet and writer

LIFE UNEDITED IS FUNNY.

SINBAD [DAVID ADKINS] (B. 1957)
American comedian

The trouble with a lot of people is they're looking for something for nothing—and it doesn't exist. You have to go out there and work for it. I don't play no lotto, no numbers and all that stuff; that ain't my cup of tea.

MATEL DAWSON, JR. (B. 1921)
American philanthropist

Those too impressed with material things cannot hold their place in the world of culture; they are relegated to inferiority and ultimate death.

ALEXANDER CRUMMELL (1819–1898)
American abolitionist

I THINK YOU DON'T NEED TO WORRY ABOUT THE ENEMY ANYMORE. YOU'D BETTER JUST WORRY ABOUT YOURSELF.

JUNE M. JORDAN (B. 1936)
American poet and social activist

Discrimination and intolerance will eat you up and destroy whatever creativity was in you if you let it.

GORDON PARKS, SR. (B. 1912)
American photographer, filmmaker, and writer

LOVE YOURSELF AND YOUR KIND.

ELIJAH MUHAMMAD (1897–1975)
American cleric, former leader of the Nation of Islam

I believe human[s] have serious value. I'm in most people's corner.

ELAINE BROWN (B. 1943)
American political activist and writer

NOBODY ROOTS FOR GOLIATH.

WILT CHAMBERLAIN (B. 1936)
American athlete

[O]nce we reach adulthood, we all have our own coulda-woulda-shouldas that we must deal with, along with a generous dose of regret.

BRAD ELLIOT
American refinery operator

EVERYONE OF US IS A WONDER. EVERYONE OF US HAS A STORY.

KRISTIN HUNTER (B. 1931)
American writer

To be who you are and become what you are capable of is the only goal worth living.

ALVIN AILEY (1931–1989)
American choreographer and dancer

If you always do what you always did, you will always get what you always got.

JACKIE "MOMS" MABLEY (1894–1975)
American entertainer

I have found thoughts and words to be the foundation for success and failure in life. I'm teaching my kids when to whisper and when to shout.

DIANA ROSS (B. 1944)

American entertainer

THEY WHO HUMBLE THEMSELVES BEFORE KNOWLEDGE OF ANY KIND GENERALLY END UP WISER—AND AS VOICES WITH SOME-THING MEANINGFUL TO SAY.

HAKI MADHUBUTTI [DON LEE] (B. 1942)

American poet, critic, publisher, and writer

The wise person speaks carefully and with truth, for every word that passes through one's teeth is meant for something.

MOLEFI KETE ASANTE (B. 1942)

American historian, educator, and writer

There are times when you are having a private conversation with someone and, unbeknownst to you, others are listening. Often the eavesdroppers will not only hear, but learn something. As a result, their thinking and behavior may be positively affected by what was, in fact, a conversation not particularly intended for them.

JOHNETTA B. COLE (B. 1936)

American educator and president of Spellman College

EVERYTHING DOVETAILS. . . . YOU HAVE NO IDEA HOW MANY KINDS OF INFORMATION, PICKED UP ONE PLACE OR ANOTHER, WILL BECOME HANDY.

LOUISE E. JEFFERSON (B. 1908)

American calligrapher, cartographer, and photographer

You can't invent events. They just happen. But you have to be prepared to deal with them when they happen.

CONSTANCE BAKER MOTTLEY (B. 1921)

American federal judge

A good head and a good heart are always a formidable combination.

NELSON MANDELA (B. 1918)

president of South Africa

It ain't what's on your head; it's what's in it.

JAMIL ABDULLAH AL-AMIN [H. RAP BROWN] (B. 1943)

American social activist and writer

YOU HAVE TO ASSESS EVERY SITUATION THAT YOU'RE IN AND HAVE TO DECIDE, IS THIS HAPPENING BECAUSE I'M BLACK? IS THIS HAPPENING BECAUSE I'M A WOMAN? OR IS THIS HAPPENING BECAUSE THIS IS HOW IT HAPPENS.

CHARLAYNE HUNTER-GAULT (B. 1942)

American journalist

The subject of race, especially to African Americans, is not something you can reduce to any card game. More important, race plays a part in everything in America if people come to grips with it.

JOHNNY L. COCHRAN, JR. (B. 1937)
American attorney

I DON'T FIT IN WITH WHITES, AND I DON'T FIT IN WITH BLACKS. WE'RE IN A MIXED-UP GENERATION, THOSE OF US WHO WERE SENT OUT TO INTEGRATE SOCIETY.

CLARENCE THOMAS (B. 1948)
American Supreme Court Justice

Whatever I do or think as a Black can never be more than a variant of what all people do and think.

SHELBY STEELE (B. 1946)
American writer

I WAS RAISED TO BELIEVE THAT EXCELLENCE IS THE BEST DETERRENT TO RACISM OR SEXISM.

OPRAH WINFREY (B. 1954)
American broadcaster and actress

You can't hold a man down without staying down with him.

BOOKER T. WASHINGTON (1856–1915)
American educator, social reformer, and writer

My job is to be resilient. That's why I call life a dance.

BILL T. JONES (B. 1952)
American choreographer and dancer

EVEN WITH THE BEST OF INTENTIONS AND A LONG-TERM STRATEGY FOR CHANGE, SUCCESS CAN BE MADDENINGLY ELUSIVE.

KURT LIDELL SCHMOKE (B. 1949)
American politician

The arc of the moral universe is long, but it bends toward justice.

THEODORE PARKER (1810–1860)
American abolitionist

PLEASE ALL AND YOU WILL PLEASE NONE.

AESOP (C. 550 B.C.)
African storyteller

I don't know the key to success, but the key to failure is trying to please everybody.

BILL COSBY (B. 1937)
American entertainer and writer

YOU CAN'T SAVE EVERYBODY.

JOE LOUIS CLARK (B. 1939)
American educator

I AM AWED AT MAN'S INGENUITY AND WHAT HE CAN ACHIEVE. I RECOGNIZED WHAT A BEAUTIFUL AND FRAGILE PLANET WE LIVE ON. SEEING EARTH FROM 170 MILES OUT IN SPACE IS NOT LIKE STANDING ON EARTH AND LOOKING AT THE MOON.

GUION BLUFORD (B. 1942)

American astronaut

Those who practice hate can only do so as long as we continue to promote it and to tolerate it.

HENRY J. LYONS

American cleric

TOO MUCH AGREEMENT KILLS A CHAT.

ELDRIDGE CLEAVER (B. 1935)

American political activist and writer

Go very light on vices such as carrying on in society. The social ramble ain't restful.

SATCHEL PAGE (1906–1982)

American athlete

I have learned that the subtle art of rejection used with finesse can be every bit as abusive as a punch in the face.

GORDON PARKS, SR. (B. 1912)

American photographer, writer, and filmmaker

SOMETIMES BEING A FRIEND MEANS MASTERING THE ART OF TIMING. THERE IS A TIME FOR SILENCE. A TIME TO LET GO AND ALLOW PEOPLE TO HURL THEMSELVES INTO THEIR OWN DESTINY. AND A TIME TO PICK UP THE PIECES WHEN IT'S ALL OVER.

GLORIA NAYLOR (B. 1950)

American writer

Mouths don't empty themselves until the ears are sympathetic and knowing.

ZORA NEALE HURSTON (1891–1960)

American writer and anthropologist

WHEN YOU CLENCH YOUR FIST, NO ONE CAN PUT ANYTHING IN YOUR HAND, NOR CAN YOU PICK UP ANYTHING.

ALEX HALEY (1921–1992)

American writer and journalist

Start by saving even a dollar a week; it adds up.

MATEL DAWSON, JR. (B. 1921)

American philanthropist

If I'd known I was going to live this long, I'd have taken better care of myself.

EUBIE BLAKE (1883–1983)

American composer

Don't buy where you can't work.

ADAM CLAYTON POWELL, JR. (1908–1972)

American cleric, politician, and civil rights leader

DON'T LOOK BACK: SOMETHING MIGHT BE GAINING ON YOU.

SATCHEL PAGE (1906–1982)

American athlete

Here's a fleeting glimpse of the heart . . . that beats and suffers for hopes—for freedom. Here's the fluid something that's like iron. Here's the real dynamite that Joe Louis uncovered!

RICHARD WRIGHT (1908–1960)

American writer

Health nuts are going to feel stupid someday, lying in hospitals dying of nothing.

REDD FOXX (1922–1991)

American comedian and actor

Without health, there can be no beauty.

NAOMI SIMMS (B. 1949)

American model

ALWAYS BE SMARTER THAN THE PEOPLE WHO HIRE YOU.

LENA HORNE (B. 1917)

American entertainer

WHY SHOULD I COMPLAIN ABOUT MAKING $7,000 A WEEK PLAY-ING A MAID? IF I DIDN'T, I'D BE MAKING $7 A WEEK BEING A MAID.

HATTIE M^cDANIEL (1895–1952)

American actress

Though a person doesn't grow up with a silver spoon in her mouth, she can still taste the good things in life.

CAROLE GIST (B. 1970)

Miss USA 1990

PEACE

WE CAN ALL STRIVE TOWARD PEACE in our lives. Much like a work in progress, only a united effort will help sustain peace in our communities.

Peace doesn't always refer to social or political issues. Keeping the peace in a marriage, among family members, or achieving inner peace are issues that also are addressed in these pages. Inner peace is particularly important. The speakers consistently say that peace starts from within. Gain it, and happiness and self-worth will follow. Peace is something we can't give or help others find until we come to know it ourselves.

Maintaining a peaceful life and home leads to serenity in the world. In other words, public peace is built in private. It is nurtured by individuals who have faith in themselves and in the basic goodness of those around them. Achieving peace isn't easy, but determination urges us in that direction.

I DON'T SEE ANY COLORS. I'M BLACK, I'LL ALWAYS BE BLACK. WHEN I STAND HERE AND LOOK AT YOU, I JUST SEE YOU AS A PERSON.

CITO GASTON
American athlete

No race has a monopoly on vice or virtue, and the worth of an individual is not related to the color of his skin.

WHITNEY MOORE YOUNG (1921–1971)
American civil rights leader

HOW BIG DOES A PERSON HAVE TO GROW DOWN IN THIS PART OF THE COUNTRY BEFORE HE'S GOING TO STAND UP AND SAY, "LET US STOP TREATING OTHER MEN AND WOMEN AND CHILDREN WITH SUCH CRUELTY JUST BECAUSE THEY ARE BORN COLORED?"

MAHALIA JACKSON (1911–1972)
American singer

I didn't choose to be a Negro. I'm all mankind. I'm balanced, a peaceful man.

RICHARD PIERCE "RICHIE" HAVENS (B. 1941)
American singer

PEACE IS COSTLY, BUT IT'S WORTH THE EXPENSE.
BAGUIRMIA PROVERB

Peace: it's wonderful.

FATHER DIVINE [GEORGE BAKER] (C. 1882–1965)
American cleric [founder of Peace Mission]

YOU CAN DRAMATIZE WAR, BUT WE DON'T YET KNOW HOW TO DRAMATIZE PEACE.
ZELMA WATSON GEORGE (B. 1930)
American scholar

We have flown the air like birds and swum the sea like fishes, but have yet to learn the simple act of walking the earth like brothers.

MARTIN LUTHER KING, JR. (1929–1968)
American minister, civil rights leader, and writer

Ah! Why will men forget that they are brethren?

BENJAMIN BANNEKER (1731–1806)
American mathematician, astronomer, and social activist

NO RACIAL OPTION NARROWS GRIEF.

COUNTEE CULLEN (B. 1903)

American writer

If the tongue and the mouth quarrel, they invariably make up because they have to live in the same head.

NIGERIAN PROVERB

SURELY PEOPLE OF GOOD WILL CAN COME TOGETHER TO SALVAGE THE WORLD.

BETTY SHABAZZ (1920—1997)

American social activist and educator [spouse of Malcolm X]

[P]ieces are lying there on the table and the challenge is to put them into one picture.

FRANKLIN SONN (B. 1941)

South African ambassador

Like jars of ginger we are sealed
By nature's heritage.

GWENDOLYN BENNETT (1902—1981)

American poet

WE MUST TURN TO EACH OTHER AND NOT ON EACH OTHER.

JESSE JACKSON (B. 1941)

American cleric and civil rights leader

WE MUST TRY TO TRUST ONE ANOTHER.

JOMO KENYATTA [KAMAU WA NEGRIL] (1891–1978)

president of Kenya and writer

We're all like blind men on a corner—we got to learn to trust people, or we'll never cross the street.

GEORGE FOREMAN (B. 1949)

American athlete

It is a good thing to be dependent on each other for something; it makes things civil and peaceable.

SOJOURNER TRUTH (C. 1791–1883)

American suffragist and abolitionist

Perhaps the time will come when it will not be necessary to shoot.

CHINUA ACHEBE (B. 1930)

Nigerian writer

THERE ARE MORE PLEASANT THINGS TO DO THAN BEAT UP PEOPLE.

MUHAMMAD ALI [CASSIUS CLAY] (B. 1952)

American athlete

I have a bias which leads me to believe that no problem of human relations is ever insoluble.

RALPH BUNCHE (1904–1971)

American political scientist and activist

LET THERE BE EVERYWHERE OUR VOICES, OUR EYES, OUR THOUGHTS, OUR LOVE, OUR ACTIONS, BREATHING HOPE AND VICTORY.

SONIA SANCHEZ (B. 1934)

American poet and educator

The spirit of Harriet Tubman, Sojourner Truth, and Frederick Douglass fill me with courage and determination that every Negro boy and girl, yes and every White boy and girl, shall walk this land, free and with dignity.

PAUL ROBESON (1898–1976)

American expatriate actor and singer

My head whirls, but now and again I remember that there is so much more to know than I am accustomed to knowing, and so much more to love than I am accustomed to loving.

JULIETTE DERRICOTTE (1897–1931)

American social activist

Love people. . . . Love people not for who or what they are, but love them.

ELLA FITZGERALD (1918–1996)

American singer

THE MEASURE OF A COUNTRY'S GREATNESS IS ITS ABILITY TO RETAIN COMPASSION IN TIMES OF CRISIS.

THURGOOD MARSHALL (1908–1993)

American Supreme Court Justice

I say that if each person in this world would simply take a small piece of this huge thing, this tablecloth, bedspread, whatever, and work it regardless of the color of the yarn, we will have harmony on this planet.

CICELY TYSON (B. 1933)

American actress

I would love to live in a world where people are valued on the basis of what qualities they have to offer as a person, rather than on the means that they happen to have at any given time.

RUTH J. SIMMONS (B. 1946)

American educator

Life is just a short walk from the cradle to the grave—and it sure behooves us to be kind to one another along the way.

ALICE CHILDRESS (B. 1920)

American poet, playwright, and writer

The price of hating other human beings is loving oneself less.

ELDRIGE CLEAVER (B. 1935)

American political activist and writer

Let us refrain form doing evil to each other, and let us love each other as brothers, as we are the same flesh and blood. . . . It is a fool who does not love himself and his people.

ELIJAH MUHAMMAD (1896–1975)

American cleric and former leader of the Nation of Islam

I HAVE SPENT OVER HALF MY LIFE TEACHING LOVE AND BROTHERHOOD, AND I FEEL THAT IT IS BETTER TO CONTINUE TO TRY AND TEACH OR LIVE EQUALITY AND LOVE THAN IT WOULD BE TO HAVE HATRED AND PREJUDICE.

ROSA PARKS (B. 1913)
American civil rights activist

Don't hate—it's too big a burden to bear.

MARTIN LUTHER KING, SR. (1899–1984)
American minister, writer, and civil rights leader

IF A DEAD TREE FALLS, IT CARRIES WITH IT A LIVE ONE.
IVORY COAST PROVERB

I leave you love.

MARY MCLEOD BETHUNE (1875–1955)
American educator and civil rights activist

THERE IS NO MEDICINE TO CURE HATRED.
AFRICAN PROVERB

One for all and all for one.

ALEXANDRE DUMAS (1824–1895)
French writer

Listening to Motown records in the sixties or dancing to hip hop music in the nineties may not lead one to question the sexual myths of Black women and men, but when White and Black kids buy the same billboard hits and laud the same athletic heroes . . . the result is often a shared cultural space where some humane interaction takes place.

CORNEL WEST (B. 1953)

American educator and writer

THE VIBRATIONS OF OUR SILENT SUFFERING ARE NOT INEFFECTIVE. THEY TOUCH AND COMMUNICATE. THEY AWAKEN AND KINDLE SYMPATHIES.

JULIA RINGWOOD COSTON

American editor and publisher

The meaning of the Street in all ways and at all times is the need for sharing life with others and the search for humanity.

VIRGINIA HAMILTON (B. 1936)

American writer

I NEVER FELT GETTING ANGRY WOULD DO ANY GOOD OTHER THAN HURT YOUR OWN DIGESTION—KEEP YOU FROM EATING, WHICH I LIKED TO DO.

SEPTIMA CLARK (1898–1987)

American civil rights activist

Stereotypes are fabricated from fragments of reality, and it is these fragments that give life, continuity, and availability for manipulation.

RALPH ELLISON (1914–1994)

American writer

If all men do not soon rise to a never before reached plateau of moral compassion and daily life based upon mutual concessions then all people will suffer the dire consequences.

CONSTANCE ELAINE BERKELEY (B. 1931)

American writer

[I] RECOGNIZE NO RIGHTS BUT HUMAN RIGHTS—I KNOW NOTHING OF MEN'S RIGHTS AND WOMEN'S RIGHTS.

ANGELINA GRIMKE (1805–1879)

American abolitionist, suffragist, and writer

I try to practice the golden rule; I believe we get out of the world what we put into it. I wish sincerely to be just to others, and I am truly humble.

CARRIE BULLOCK

American nurse

The only way to make sure people you agree with can speak is to support the rights of people you don't agree with.

ELEANOR HOLMES NORTON (B. 1937)

American attorney

LESS THEOLOGY AND MORE OF HUMAN BROTHERHOOD, LESS DECLAMATION AND MORE COMMON SENSE AND LOVE AND TRUTH, MUST BE THE QUALIFICATIONS OF THE NEW MINISTRY THAT SHALL YET SAVE THE RACE FROM THE EVILS OF FALSE TEACHINGS.

FANNIE BARRIER WILLIAMS (1855–1944)

American social activist

The life of a nation is secure only while that nation is honest, truthful, and virtuous.

FREDERICK DOUGLASS (C. 1817–1895)

American abolitionist and writer

[T]HE HISTORIES OF BLACKS AND JEWS, IN BONDAGE AND OUT OF BONDAGE, HAVE BEEN BLOOD HISTORIES PURSUED THROUGH OUR KINDRED SEARCHINGS FOR SELF-DETERMINATION. LET THIS BLOOD BE A STAIN OF HONOR THAT WE SHARE. LET US NOT NOW BECOME ENEMIES TO OURSELVES AND TO EACH OTHER.

JUNE JORDAN (B. 1936)

American poet and social activist

We have to think about other people of color in a global sense and the relationship not just between Whites and people of color, but among and within communities of color.

CAROL LANI GUINIER (B. 1950)

American lawyer and educator

POLITICS

MAKING THINGS POSSIBLE IS the unifying theme to the political messages here. Feeding the hungry, making dreams come true, housing the poor—these are political concerns, say the voices in this chapter.

These voices have little faith in the integrity of politicians, but they believe that our participation in the political system will help fulfill its best intentions, thus assuring that every citizen has a voice in the activities of government. Forthright and direct, the speakers here do not encourage us to look to government for our basic needs, but rather to take hold of government until it serves the interests of everyone.

In this chapter, the personal becomes political. How we treat each other can have a positive impact on how different communities interact with one another. It also can affect how governments treat their citizens. The voices here call to us across political lines and insist that serving one another isn't something we should leave to our politicians. It's a job we should adopt ourselves.

WE PREFER THE POVERTY IN FREEDOM TO RICHES IN SLAVERY.

SEKOU TOURE (1922—1984)

President of Guinea

The real question, the all commanding question, is whether American justice, American liberty, American civilization, American law, and American Christianity can be made to include and protect alike and forever all American citizens.

FREDERICK DOUGLASS (C. 1817—1895)

American abolitionist and writer

THERE WAS SO MUCH PRESSURE TO ACCEPT THAT INTEGRATION WAS WONDERFUL—OUR PARENTS TOLD US IT WAS, OUR LEADERS TOLD US IT WAS.

NA'IM AKBAR (B. 1944)

American psychologist

You get a couple of preachers, the next step is to have a bunch of honky social workers. Next thing you know they done fixed the street, put in new sewers, built a new school, an' raised taxes. There goes the damned neighborhood.

DAVID BRADLEY (B. 1947)

American writer

The question of love is irrelevant . . . political communities are not based upon principles of love but of certain principles of justice.

E. FRANKLIN FRAZIER (1894—1962)

American sociologist and educator

IT SEEMS TO ME THAT WE FIRST HAVE TO UNDERSTAND THAT RACISM IS PERMANENT, AND THAT WE HAVE TO TAKE A STANCE.

DERRICK BELL (B. 1930)

American law professor and educator

Any demand that victims of oppression be required to love those who oppress them places an additional and probably intolerable psychological burden upon these victims.

KENNETH B. CLARKE (B. 1914)

American sociologist

If they come for me in the morning, they will come for you at night.

ANGLEA Y. DAVIS (B. 1944)

American civil rights activist, writer, and educator

People are people. And government is government.

GLORIA NAYLOR (B. 1950)

American writer

NO RACE, NO NATION, NO MAN HAS ANY DIVINE RIGHT TO TAKE ADVANTAGE OF OTHERS.

MARCUS GARVEY (1887—1940)

Jamaican social activist

[B]lack folks have been in the forefront of the struggle against American racism. If these efforts fall prey to anti-Semitism, then the principled attempt to combat racism forfeits much of its moral credibility—and we all lose.

CORNEL WEST (B. 1953)

American educator and writer

AS WITH THE JEW, DISCRIMINATION IS MAKING THE NEGRO INTERNATIONAL.

ALAIN LOCKE (1886—1954)

American scholar, educator, and writer

Any glorification of Black that brings about cruelty is bad.

STERLING A. BROWN (B. 1901)

American writer

THE FOREMOST ENEMY OF THE NEGRO INTELLIGENTSIA HAS BEEN ISOLATION.

LORRAINE HANSBERRY (1930—1965)

American playwright

We have marginalized ourselves because we don't vote. . . . We did that to ourselves by not participating and leaving public policy without much input from minority voices.

CYNTHIA MCKINNEY

American politician

It is a narrow nationalism that says the white man is the enemy. . . . Nationalism, so-called when it says "all non-blacks are our enemy," is sickness or criminality, in fact, a form of fascism.

IMAMU AMIRI BARAKA [LEROI JONES] (B. 1934)

American writer

What could be more absurd and ridiculous than that one group of individuals who are trying to throw off the yoke of oppression themselves, so as to get relief from conditions, which handicap and injure them, should favor laws and customs which impede the progress of another unfortunate group and hinder them in every conceivable way?

MARY CHURCH TERRELL (1863—1954)

American educator and social reformer

Anyone who wants to take this country forward has to be willing to make the workplace a level playing field.

SHEILA JACKSON LEE
American politician

A SURE WAY FOR ONE TO LIFT HIMSELF UP IS BY HELPING TO LIFT SOMEONE ELSE.

BOOKER T. WASHINGTON (1856—1915)
American educator, social reformer, and writer

If you're going to hold someone down, you're going to have to hold onto the other end of the chain. You are confined by your own system of repression.

TONI MORRISON (B. 1931)
American writer

Only equals can be friends.

ETHIOPIAN PROVERB

NO MATTER HOW MUCH RESPECT, NO MATTER HOW MUCH RECOG-NITION, WHITES SHOW TOWARDS ME, AS FAR AS I'M CONCERNED, AS LONG AS IT IS NOT SHOWN TO EVERY ONE OF OUR PEOPLE IN THIS COUNTRY, IT DOESN'T EXIST FOR ME.

EL-HAJJ MALIK EL-SHABAZZ [MALCOLM X] (1925—1965)
American cleric and civil rights activist

Our highest ambition is to be included in the stream of American life, to be permitted to "play the game" as any other American; and it is opposed to anything that aids in the exclusion; the face may be Africa, but the heart has the beat of Wall Street.

CHESTER HIMES (1909—1984)
American expatriate writer

QUESTION EVERYTHING. EVERY STRIPE, EVERY STAR, EVERY WORD SPOKEN. QUESTION EVERYTHING.

ERNEST GAINES (B. 1933)
American writer

The heft we carry on the basketball courts and football fields, the brawn and boldness in the boxing rings, does not translate into political heft. For too long we have been victims of political circumstance, and our failures of political will have left us standing at the levee, beholden to the roustabouts, and pontificating on the virtues of poverty and victimization.

AUGUST WILSON (B. 1945)
American playwright

I DO TAKE A RELATIVELY SCIENTIFIC APPROACH TO POLITICS . . . I ALWAYS DO RESEARCH. PEOPLE DON'T ALWAYS TELL YOU THE WHOLE STORY, SO YOU HAVE TO RESEARCH.

ETHEL D. ALLEN (1929—1981)
American physician, politician, and social activist

WE DON'T WANT PEOPLE TO DO POLICE WORK. WE WANT THEM TO BE OUR EYES AND EARS.

LEE P. BROWN (B. 1937)

American cabinet member and New York City police commissioner

The intellectuals must gain respect through their efficiency, their for unselfish work on behalf of the people, and their clarity.

CHEIKH ANTA DIOP (B. 1923—1986)

Senegalese historian

POLITICS WAS THE ONE WAY TO MAKE THINGS EASIER, TO BE AT THE TABLE, TO STIR THE SOUP A LITTLE YOURSELF.

HARVEY GRANT (B. 1943)

American politician

Wherever there is chaos, it creates wonderful thinking. Chaos is a gift.

SEPTIMA CLARK (1898—1987)

American civil rights activist

HE WHO CONTROLS IMAGES CONTROLS EVERYTHING.

ROBERT TOWNSHEND (B. 1957)

American actor and filmmaker

Democracy without housing, health and food is meaningless.

LINDIWE MABUZA (B. 1939)

South African linguist and ambassador to Germany

If we were to step out of our xenophobia and become true democrats, with a small *d*, we would realize that we are not a premier democracy and that we have a lot to learn from other democracies around the world, where twice as many citizens compared to the United States participate in elections.

CAROL LANI GUINIER (B. 1950)
American lawyer and educator

A DEMOCRACY CANNOT LONG ENDURE WITH THE HEAD OF A GOD AND THE TAIL OF A DEMON.

JOSEPHINE YATES
American writer

I have cherished the idea of a democratic and free society . . . [it] is an idea for which I'm prepared to die.

NELSON MANDELA (B. 1918)
President of South Africa

DEMOCRACY IS NOT TOLERANCE. DEMOCRACY IS A PRESCRIBED WAY OF LIFE ERECTED ON THE PREMISE THAT ALL MEN ARE CREATED EQUAL.

CHESTER HIMES (1909—1984)
American expatriate writer

MY FAITH IN THE CONSTITUTION IS WHOLE, IT IS COMPLETE, IT IS TOTAL. I AM NOT GOING TO SIT HERE AND BE AN IDLE SPECTATOR TO THE DIMINUTION, THE SUBVERSION, THE DESTRUCTION OF THE CONSTITUTION.

BARBARA JORDAN (B. 1936)
American politician and educator

When you have a law, you have an instrument that will work for you permanently.

CLARENCE MAURICE, JR. (1911—1984)
American lawyer and lobbyist

As far as I'm concerned, you're not going to change the hearts and minds. You have to change the law.

YVONNE BRATHWAITE BURKE (B. 1932)
American politician

You get things done a lot faster when you're wired into the corporate community.

SYBIL COLLINS MOBLEY (B. 1925)
American educator

OUR ONLY HOPE IS TO CONTROL THE VOTE.

MEDGAR WILEY EVARS (1926—1963)
American civil rights activist

THE SYSTEM IS DESIGNED TO DELAY DECISION MAKING—TO INVEST MORE IN PROCESS THAN RESULTS.

WILLIE L. BROWN, JR. (B. 1934)

American politician

Racism . . . asserts that one group has the stigmata of superiority and the other has those of inferiority. . . . For racism is an *ism* to which everyone in the world today is exposed; for or against, we must take sides. And the history of the future will differ according to the decision we make.

RUTH BENEDICT (1887—1948)

American scientist and writer

IN ORDER TO BE A GOOD LEADER, ONE MUST HAVE SKILLFULLY MASTERED THE ART OF COMPASSION.

SHARON PRATT DIXON (B. 1944)

American politician

I say leadership is good when you don't overstep it, you can lead and then be able to follow at times.

RUBY MIDDLETON FORSYTHE (B. 1905)

American teacher

Everything can be explained to the people, on the single condition that you really want them to understand.

FRANTZ FANON (1925—1961)

Martinique-born Algerian psychiatrist and writer

Most power is illusionary and perceptual. You have to create an environment in which people perceive you as having some power.

CARRIE SAXON PERRY (B. 1931)
American politician

Leadership should be born out of the understanding of the needs of those who would be affected by it.

MARIAN ANDERSON (1902—1993)
American singer

[T]OO MUCH PAPERWORK, NOT ENOUGH PEOPLE WORK.

LEAH J. SEARS-COLLINS (B. 1955)
American lawyer and state supreme justice

The artist and the political activist are one. They are both shapers of the future reality. Both understand and manipulate the collective myths of the race. Both are warriors, priests, lovers, and destroyers.

LARRY NEAL (1937—1981)
American poet

The air has finally gotten to the place that we can breathe it together.

SEPTIMA CLARK (1898—1987)
American educator and civil rights activist

RESPONSIBILITY

PEOPLE WHO STRIVE FOR SOCIAL CHANGE are often mistaken for wanting the world handed to them on a silver platter. Some believe they are looking for privileges they haven't earned.

None of the speakers here have much tolerance for people seeking a hand-out, or for anyone unwilling to work toward improving society. In this chapter, whether you've got plenty or nothing at all, the responsibility for your destiny is your own. But that doesn't mean we shouldn't help and support those in need.

There is a sense that the very definition of "humanity" is linked to becoming our brother's keeper—looking out for his interests, since they are our own. The messages here don't resemble the old, glib, bitter refrains about picking yourself up by the boot straps. The speakers in this section have something more compassionate and useful in mind. They are asking us to take responsibility for ourselves and one another, so that we can concentrate on the things we share in common rather than on what pulls us apart.

WE [AFRICAN AMERICANS] CAN'T WALK AWAY FROM THE REST OF AMERICA AND GO OFF INTO OUR OWN LITTLE WORLD.

COLIN L. POWELL (B. 1937)
American military officer and former chairman of Joint Chiefs of Staff

He who can do nothing, does nothing.
GAMBIAN PROVERB

THE FUTURE MUST BE PLANNED TODAY. WE MAY NEVER SEE IT IN OUR LIFETIME, BUT THE SUCCESS OF OUR VENTURES WILL IMPACT FUTURE GENERATIONS.

L. DOUGLASS WILDER (B. 1931)
American politician

The young cannot teach tradition to the old.
NIGERIAN PROVERB

It is time for everyone of us to roll up our sleeves and put ourselves at the top of our commitment list.

MARIAN WRIGHT EDELMAN (B. 1939)
American attorney and founder of the Children's Defense League

DO YOU ASK WHAT WE CAN DO? UNITE AND BUILD A STORE OF YOUR OWN. . . . DO YOU ASK WHERE IS THE MONEY? WE HAVE SPENT MORE THAN ENOUGH ON FOOLISHNESS.

MARIA W. STEWART (1803—1879)
American abolitionist

When you have opportunity in life you are obligated to give something back.

PATRICIA L. IRVIN
American lawyer

WE ARE RESPONSIBLE FOR THE WORLD IN WHICH WE FIND OUR-SELVES, IF ONLY BECAUSE WE ARE THE ONLY SENTIENT FORCE WHICH CAN CHANGE IT.

JAMES BALDWIN (1924—1987)
American writer

One must always be aware, to notice—even though the cost of notic-ing is to become responsible.

THYLIAS MOSS
American artist

Each effort won't be a great effort
    but each effort should be your best
In order to gain the most from your ability
    and hopefully attain success
        love, peace, and happiness.

OTIS SMITH (B. 1939)
American poet and lecturer

THE RACE NEEDS DARING, ORIGINAL PEOPLE TO THINK AND SPEAK.

EMMA AZALIA SMITH HACKLEY (1867—1922)
American singer

Every people should be the originators of their own designs. The projectors of their own schemes, and creators of events that lead to their destiny—the consummation of their desires.

MARTIN R. DELANEY (1812—1885)
American editor, abolitionist, soldier, and writer

FELLOW CITIZENS, RIGHTS IMPOSE DUTIES.

ROBERT B. ELLIOT (1842—1884)
American politician

Without discipline, true freedom cannot survive.

KWAME NKRUMAH (1902—1972)
president of Ghana and co-Head of State of Guinea

There is no such thing as freedom without discipline. The one who is free is disciplined.

JANET COLLINS (B. 1923)
American dancer and prima ballerina

[D]iscipline establishes the format, the environment for academic achievement to occur.

JOE LOUIS CLARK (B. L939)
American educator

LIVING AND DYING IS NOT THE BIG ISSUE. THE BIG ISSUE IS WHAT YOU'RE GOING TO DO WITH YOUR TIME WHILE YOU'RE HERE.

BILL T. JONES (B. 1952)
American choreographer and dancer

Live free and leave a print on history.

HERMAN K. HARRIS (B. 1940)
American educator

IT IS THE CHALLENGE TO USE ONE'S LIFE IN A WAY THAT RE-SPONDS TO THE EVILS IN YOUR MIDST. THAT IS WHAT WE ALL MUST DO.

DERRICK BELL (B. 1930)
American law professor and writer

The thing that I have done throughout my life is to do the best job that I can to be me . . . I really feel like I'm a role model, what I'd like to be is someone who says, "No, don't try necessarily to be like me or . . . to be an astronaut or a physician unless that's what you want to do."

MAE C. JAMISON (B. 1957)
American astronaut

WHEN I WAS A HONKY-TONK ENTERTAINER, I USED TO WORK FROM NINE TO UNCONSCIOUS.

ETHEL WATERS (1896—1977)
American actress

Maybe the worst somebody could ever say of me was: He was fairly undiplomatic in the way to get things done. But at least he tried to get things done.

BRYANT GUMBEL (B. 1948)
American journalist

MY MOTHER TRIED AND SHE TRIED. SHE DID NOT HAVE ANY HELP. SHE COULD NOT GET ANY CHILD CARE. SHE COULD NOT GET A JOB. SHE COULD NOT GET ANY TRAINING, BUT SHE TRIED.

MAXINE WATERS (B. 1938)
American politician

Was he the only fisherman left in the world
using the old ways, who believed his work was prayer,
who caught only enough, since the sea had to live.

DEREK WALCOTT (B. 1930)

St. Lucian poet

Advertising is the single most important way of reaching everyone in
America, and I feel a deep sense of responsibility for my work.

BARBARA GARDNER PROCTOR (B. 1933)

American advertising executive

[A] SENSE OF RESPONSIBILITY WHICH COMES WITH POWER IS THE RAREST OF THINGS.

ALEXANDER CRUMMELL (1819—1898)

American cleric, educator, and writer

Let the Afro-American depend on no party, but on himself for his salvation. Let him continue toward education, character, and above
all, put money in his purse.

IDA B. WELLS (1862—1931)

American journalist, civil rights activist, and educator

UNLESS A SENSE OF SERVICE AND DUTY IS INSTILLED, OUR UPWARD MOBILITY WILL ONLY BE MEASURED BY CARS AND STYLING.

NIARA SUDARKASA [GLORIA MARSHALL] (B. 1938)

American educator

REVOLUTION

NEARLY EVERY CHAPTER OF THIS BOOK has qualities that might be described as "revolutionary." This isn't because the speakers all share a similar political ideology or social agenda. In fact, if all the speakers in this book were put together in a room, it's likely they'd find little to agree upon. But all would be determined to assert their views of the world—and that is what makes each one a revolutionary.

Silence equals collaboration in this chapter, participation in one's own demise. Speaking out and raising the issues is the first step in effecting positive social change, joining in what novelist Lorene Cary has called "an unruly conversation." What makes it unruly is that diplomacy is often checked at the door, and the urgency of the subject matter dictates the tone of the discussion. Those who are part of the problem rather than part of the solution are easy to identify—they are the ones who keep their mouths shut or keep their voices low.

The most resonant voices—here and in society in general—are those that speak to the necessity of a revolution in the hearts and minds of all of us. This revolution, according to Dr. King and others, is one in which we look past our differences in order to find the qualities we share in common. Together these voices become unified, crying out, "We want to be free!"

WHEN REFORM BECOMES IMPOSSIBLE, REVOLUTION BECOMES IMPERATIVE.

KELLY MILLER (1863—1939)
American sociologist and educator

One does not glorify in romanticizing revolution. One cries.
LORRAINE HANSBERRY (1930—1965)
American playwright

Win or lose, we will win by raising the issues.
CHARLOTTA SPEARS BASS (1890—1969)
American journalist, publisher, and political activist

WE'RE GOING TO DO OUR PART, AND WE WILL WIN, BECAUSE WE ARE ON GOD'S SIDE.

JOE LOUIS (1914—1981)

American athlete

The law cannot do it for us. We must do for ourselves.

SHIRLEY CHISHOLM (B. 1924)

American politician and first black congresswoman

We declare here today in no uncertain terms that the path of progress has been filled with pain and suffering and sacrifice, and that we're fed up and fired up. . . . We don't intend to sit by and watch the meager gains washed away by a flood tide of insidious insensitivity nor invidious individualism. . . . In other words, we ain't going back.

JOSEPH LOWERY (B. 1924)

American cleric and president of the Southern Christian Leadership Conference

The panther is a fierce animal, but he will not attack until he is backed into a corner; then he will strike out.

HUEY NEWTON (1942—1989)

American political activist and co-founder of the Black Panther Party

I SAY VIOLENCE IS NECESSARY. IT IS AS AMERICAN AS CHERRY PIE.

JAMIL ABDULLAH AL-AMIN [H. RAP BROWN] (B. 1943)

American political activist and writer

[U]norganized violence is like a blind man with a pistol.

CHESTER HIMES (1909—1984)

American expatriate writer

HATRED SHOOK HER AS A STRONG WIND SHAKES A BOUGHLESS TREE.

J. SAUNDERS REDDING (1906—1988)

American educator and writer

He who makes you pay in tears, make him pay in blood.

MASAI PROVERB

AGITATORS ARE INEVITABLE. THEY ARE AS NECESSARY TO SOCIAL ORGANISM AS BLOOD IS TO ANIMAL ORGANISM. REVOLUTION FOLLOWS AS A MATTER OF COURSE.

T. THOMAS FORTUNE (1856—1928)

American journalist and editor

Let your motto be resistance! Resistance! RESISTANCE! No oppressed people have ever secured their liberty without resistance.

HENRY H. GARNET (1815—1882)

American educator, abolitionist, and diplomat

Just like a tree that's standing by the water,
    We shall not be moved.

AFRICAN-AMERICAN SPIRITUAL

History says we can and will survive if we do what our spiritual tells us: Keep your hand on the plow, hold on.

LERONE BENNETT (B. 1928)

American editor, historian, and scholar

In . . . struggle our watchword needs to be, "Work, work, work!" and our rallying cry, "Fight, fight, fight!"

JAMES WELDON JOHNSON (1871—1938)

American educator, poet, social activist, and writer

We will either find a way, or make one.

HANNIBAL (247 B.C.–C. 183–181)

North African military leader

While I had been fighting in Vietnam alongside brave soldiers trying to preserve their freedom, in my own land a simmering conflict had turned into an open fight in our streets and cities—a fight that had to be won.

COLIN L. POWELL (B. 1937)

American military officer and former chairman of the Joint Chiefs of Staff

WE REFUSE TO BELIEVE THIS COUNTRY, SO POWERFUL TO DEFEND ITS CITIZENS ABROAD, IS UNABLE TO PROTECT ITS CITIZENS AT HOME.

IDA B. WELLS (1862—1931)

American journalist, educator, and civil rights activist

I REALIZE NOW THAT I HAD TO FIGHT FOR THE MORAL AND POLITICAL HEALTH OF AMERICA AS A WHOLE AND FOR HER POSITION IN THE WORLD AT LARGE.

MARIAN WRIGHT EDELMAN (B. 1939)

American lawyer and founder of the Children's Defense League

There was only one thing I could do—hammer relentlessly, continually crying aloud, even if in a wilderness, and force open, by sheer muscle, every closed door.

ADAM CLAYTON POWELL, JR. (1908—1972)

American cleric, politician, and civil rights leader

I can no longer bear what I have borne.

MARTIN PROSSER (B. 1936)

American writer

OUR LIVES, OUR HOPES AND DREAMS DEPEND ON OUR ABILITY TO BE HEARD.

JAMES BERNARD (B. 1965)

American editor and writer

When it comes to the cause of justice, I take no prisoners and I don't believe in compromising.

MARY FRANCES BERRY (B. 1938)

American scholar

I am not sick. I am broken.

FRIDA KAHLO (1903—1954)

American painter

SURVIVAL AIN'T LIBERATION.

KESHO YVONNE SCOTT

American writer

You don't stick a knife in a man's back nine inches and then pull it out six inches and say you're making progress.

EL-HAJJ MALIK EL-SHABAZZ [MALCOLM X] (1925—1965)

American cleric and civil rights activist

[T]HE WHITE MENTALITY [HAS] CREATED A FOOL'S PARADISE FOR THEMSELVES.

WINNIE MANDELA (B. 1934)

South African social activist

The time is always right to do what is right.

MARTIN LUTHER KING, JR. (1929—1968)

American minister, civil rights leader, and writer

PATIENCE HAS ITS LIMITS. TAKE IT TOO FAR AND IT'S COWARDICE.

GEORGE JACKSON (1942—1971)

American political activist and writer

Never say: Let well enough alone.

JOHN HOPE (1868—1936)

American educator

We have been cooling off for one hundred years.

JAMES L. FARMER (B. 1920)

American social reformer

A man is either free or he is not. There cannot be any apprentice-ship for freedom.

IMANU AMIRI BARAKA [EVERETT LEROI JONES] (B. 1934)

American poet, playwright, and writer

YOU MAY PERHAPS THINK HARD OF US FOR RUNNING AWAY FROM SLAVERY, BUT AS TO MYSELF, I HAVE BUT ONE APOLOGY TO MAKE FOR IT . . . THAT I DIDN'T START AT AN EARLIER PERIOD. I MIGHT HAVE BEEN FREE LONG BEFORE I WAS.

HENRY BIBB (1815—1854)

American journalist and abolitionist

FREEDOM HAS NEVER BEEN FREE . . . I WOULD DIE, AND DIE GLADLY, IF THAT WOULD MAKE A BETTER LIFE FOR [MY FAMILY.]

MEDGAR WYLIE EVERS (1925—1963)

American civil rights activist

Oh, freedom! Oh, freedom!
    Oh, freedom over me!
And before I'd be a slave, I'll be buried in my grave,
And go home to my Lord and be free.

AFRICAN-AMERICAN SPIRITUAL

THERE WAS ONE OR TWO THINGS I HAD A RIGHT TO, LIBERTY OR DEATH. IF I COULD NOT HAVE ONE I SHOULD HAVE THE OTHER, FOR NO MAN SHOULD TAKE ME ALIVE.

HARRIET TUBMAN (C. 1831—1913)
American abolitionist

The real radical is that person who has a vision of equality and is willing to do those things that will bring reality closer to that vision. . . . In such a social order there will no longer be walls, representing fear and insecurity, to separate people from one another.

BAYARD RUSTIN (1910—1987)
American social reformer

The close links forged between Africans and people of African descent over half a century of common struggle continue to inspire and strengthen us. For although the outward forms of our struggle may change, it remains in essence the same, a fight to death against oppression, racism, and exploitation.

KWAME NKRUMAH (1902—1972)
President of Ghana and co-Head of State of Guinea

I do not wish to be free, yet I should be glad, if others, especially the young Negroes, were to be free.

JUPITER HAMMOND (1711—1806)

American poet and cleric

There is no easy walk to freedom.

NELSON MANDELA (B. 1918)

president of South Africa

Freedom is never given; it's won.

A. PHILLIP RANDOLPH (1889—1979)

American social reformer

AMERICA IS ME. IT GAVE ME THE ONLY LIFE I KNOW SO I MUST SHARE IN ITS SURVIVAL.

GORDON PARKS, SR. (B. 1912)

American photographer, writer, and filmmaker

THIS LAND WHICH WE HAVE WATERED WITH OUR TEARS AND OUR BLOOD, IS NOW OUR MOTHER COUNTRY AND WE ARE WELL SATIS-FIED TO STAY WHERE WISDOM ABOUNDS AND THE GOSPEL IS FREE.

RICHARD ALLEN (1760—1831)

American cleric

[T]HIS GREAT NATION OF OURS, BORN IN REVOLUTION AND BLOOD, "CONCEIVED IN LIBERTY, AND DEDICATED TO THE PROPOSITION THAT ALL MEN ARE CREATED EQUAL" WILL TRULY BECOME THE LIGHTHOUSE OF FREEDOM. . . .

BENJAMIN E. MAYS (1895–1984)
American theologian, educator, and social reformer

AS WE TURN OUR FULL ATTENTION TO THE HEARTS AND MINDS OF MEN, WE SHALL SEE THAT IF A MAN CAN FLY—HE CAN ALSO BE FREE.

LORRAINE HANSBERRY (1930–1965)
American playwright

Opportunity follows struggle. It follows effort. It follows hard work. It doesn't come before.

SHELBY STEELE (B. 1946)
American writer

[P]rogress in the enjoyment of all the privileges that will come to us must be the result of severe and constant struggle rather than an artificial longing.

BOOKER T. WASHINGTON (1856–1915)
American educator, social reformer, and writer

Prejudice is like a hair across your cheek. You keep brushing at it because the feeling of it is irritating.

MARIAN ANDERSON (1902—1993)
American singer

YOU KNOW AS WELL AS I, OLD WIFE, THAT WE HAVE NOT BEEN SCUFFLING IN THIS WASTE-HOWLING WILDERNESS FOR THE RIGHT TO BE STUPID.

TONI CADE BAMBARA (1939—1995)
American writer

Lifting as they climb, onward and upward they go, struggling and striving and hoping that the buds and blossoms of their desires burst into glorious fruition ere long.

MARY CHURCH TERRELL (1863—1954)
American educator and social reformer

[M]y sitting here now is the result of people, Black people and people of good conscience in particular, fighting a struggle in the real world, changing the real attitudes and the real social situation.

DANNY GLOVER (B. 1948)
American actor

STRUGGLE IS THE FRICTION THAT HOLDS BLACK PEOPLE TOGETHER.

SEPTIMA CLARK (1898—1987)
American civil rights activist

And although it is difficult to imagine our nation totally free of racism or sexism, my intellect, my heart and my experience tell me that it is actually possible. For that day when neither exists we must all struggle.

JAMES BALDWIN (1924—1987)

American writer

I WOULD HOPE THAT [PEOPLE] CAN RELATE TO AND BE MOTIVATED BY MY THOUGHTS ON HOW IMPORTANT IT IS FOR US TO DEVELOP A PLAN OF ACTION IN TERMS OF LIBERATING OURSELVES AS A PEOPLE. . . .

ASSATA SHAKUR

American expatriate, civil rights activist, and Black Panther

SPIRITUALITY

IN THIS CHAPTER—AS IN OTHERS—VOICES are raised in unison to give testimony.

Testimonials bear witness to the goodness that exists in the world. They assert that goodness prevails even in the face of devastating challenges and hardships.

Testifying is an invisible force boiling up in our blood and propelling us toward an inevitable release. It prompts us to call out in an unexpectedly joyful voice that comes from a place in our hearts we didn't know existed. Our actions are proof that a spirit larger than ourselves touches our lives in an invisible way. That spirit threads our lives, souls, and bodies together in a colorful tapestry.

Spirituality transcends language and can't be seen or touched, but it manages to still function in our lives in meaningful ways.

Many of the speakers here point out that spirituality is not necessarily an independent system of faith devoted to a single deity. Spirituality is not of the body or the mind. It continually defies explanation and rests in the chambers of our hearts rather than in the palm of our hands.

EVERY HUMAN PERSONALITY IS SACRED POTENTIALLY DIVINE. NOBODY IS ANY MORE THAN THAT AND NOBODY CAN BE ANY LESS.

MARGARET ABIGAIL WALKER (B. 1915)

American writer

The potential for strength endurance, courage, inventiveness, and creativity exists in every human being God created.

MICHELLE WALLACE (B. 1950)

American writer and social critic

Lord, make me so uncomfortable that I will do the very thing I fear.

RUBY DEE (B. 1924)

American actress and social activist

Faith gives us the courage to take the right steps in the right direction.

SUSAN TAYLOR (B. 1946)

American journalist, editor, and writer

I try to explain to them that all they see around us, the things we have, are not of my doing. I am not the reason we have these things. God is. I want them to realize that you don't have to stab anybody in the back. You don't have to scratch anybody's eyes out. Just be honest, work hard, and have faith. That will take them further in life than anything.

DENZEL WASHINGTON (B. 1955)

American actor

Suffering breeds character. Character breeds faith. In the end faith will not disappoint.

JESSE JACKSON (B. 1941)

American cleric and civil rights leader

Your power is your faith,
Deep it and pass it to other bloods.

MOLEFI KETE ASANTE (B. 1942)

American, historian, educator and writer

"FOR GOD SO LOVED THE WORLD THAT HE GAVE HIS ONLY BE-GOTTEN SON, THAT WHOSOEVER BELIEVETH IN HIM SHOULD NOT PERISH, BUT HAVE EVERLASTING LIFE. . . ." THESE WORDS STORED UP A BATTERY OF FAITH AND CONFIDENCE AND DETERMINATION IN MY HEART WHICH HAS NOT FAILED ME TO THIS DAY.

MARY MCLEOD BETHUNE (1875–1955)

American educator, civil rights leader, and co-founder of Bethune-Cookman College

IF YOU HAVE FAITH IN GOD, IT IS AMAZING HOW [CRITICISMS] DO NOT AFFECT YOU.

SHIRLEY CHISHOLM (B. 1925)

American politician and first black congresswoman

Testimony is an integral part of the Black religious tradition. It is the occasion where the believer stands before the community of faith in order to give account of the hope that is in him or her.

JAMES CONE (B. 1938)

American theologian

When one is in trouble, one remembers God.

NIGERIAN PROVERB

GOD DON'T COME WHEN YOU WANT HIM, BUT HE'S ALWAYS RIGHT ON TIME.

AFRICAN AMERICAN PROVERB

I cannot see everything, but nothing escapes God.

TOUSSAINT L' OUVERTURE (1743–1803)

Haitian leader

We can endure almost anything if we are centered, if we have some focus in our life.

RENITA WEEMS

American cleric, writer, and educator

'Twant me—'twas the Lord. I always told Him, 'I trust you. I don't know where to go or what to do, but I expect you to lead me,' and he always did.

HARRIET TUBMAN (c. 1820–1913)

American abolitionist

ONLY GOD HAS KEPT THE NEGRO SANE.

FANNIE LOU HAMER (1917–1977)

American civil rights activist

I believe in prayer. It's the best way to draw strength from Heaven.

JOSEPHINE BAKER (1906–1975)

American-born French entertainer

There is no god like one's throat; we have to sacrifice to it every day.

NIGERIAN PROVERB

THERE ISN'T A CERTAIN TIME WE SHOULD SET ASIDE TO TALK ABOUT GOD. GOD IS PART OF OUR EVERY WAKING MOMENT.

MARVA NETTLES COLLINS (B. 1936)

American educator

We are not here to do you any harm. We merely want to have a world of prayer at this place where our ancestors were brought and sold as slaves, to ask God to help us end slavery in all its forms.

ANDRE YOUNG (B. 1932)

American cleric, civil rights activist, and politician

If Hell is what we are taught it is, then there will be more Christians there than all the days of creation.

MARCUS GARVEY (1887–1940)
Jamaican social activist

THE GOD I PRAY TO IS AS UNIVERSAL AS THE MOON IS UNIVERSAL.
DICK GREGORY (B. 1932)
American writer, humorist, and entrepreneur

[O]ur Creator is the same and never changes despite the names given Him by the people here and in all parts of the world.

GEORGE WASHINGTON CARVER (1864–1943)
American scientist and educator

YOU CANNOT ESCAPE GOD. YOU WILL MEET HIM IN FOREIGN LANDS.
NAMIBIAN PROVERB

The first of us who came flocking to your religion came there as if to a revelation—that's it, as a revelation of your secret, the secret of your power, the power of your aeroplanes, your railways, and so on. Instead of that, you started to talk to them about God, the soul of the eternal life, and so forth. Do you think they didn't know about that already long before you arrival?

MONGO BETI [ALEXANDRE BIYIDI] (B. 1932)
Cameroonian writer

MY OPPOSITION [TO APARTHEID] IS BASED FIRMLY AND SQUARELY ON THE BIBLE AND ON ANY INJUNCTIONS OF THE CHRISTIAN GOSPEL.

BISHOP DESMOND TUTU (B. 1931)
South African cleric and social activist

Everybody talkin' 'bout goin' to Heaven ain't goin' there.
AFRICAN-AMERICAN PROVERB

The argument that man may pray for what he receives, is a mistake. . . . There are no people more religious in this country, than the colored people, and none so poor and miserable than they.
MARTIN DELANEY (1812–1885)
American journalist, writer, and political activist

ANTI-SEMITISM IS A DISEASE OF EUROPE AND WHITE CHRISTIANITY. AND AFRO-AMERICAN VICTIMS OF THE FIERY CROSS MUST NOT BE DRAGGED INTO THE VORTEX OF ANTI-SEMITISM.

CLAUDE McKAY (1891–1948)
American poet

Religion without humanity is a poor human stuff.
SOJOURNER TRUTH (1797–1883)
American abolitionist

I'm beginning to think that real artists are basically religious figures. Real artists . . . are people who are compelled, are driven by their vision to produce creative work out of their souls. If you think of them as religious people, then they are driven by a need to enlighten man.

KATHLEEN COLLINS (1942–1988)

American author

All of us are seeking, in many fitful ways, to be agents of the kingdom.

BISHOP DESMOND TUTU (B. 1931)

South African cleric and social activist

For me, being a spiritual woman means looking to myself and others, but I've got to go beyond the self. . . . We can focus so closely on ourselves and forget that to be spiritual means to be connected to others.

GLORIA WADE-GAYLES

American educator and writer

GIVE IT FOR THE SAKE OF GOD, AND GIVE IT EVEN TO HIM WHO DOES NOT BELIEVE IN GOD.

BENIN PROVERB

Happiness is striving to make the other fellow happy in any manner you can. Never envy the other fellow for his good fortune. Look about you. You also have been given something. Be thankful for that which you have.

LIONEL L. THORNHILL (1897–19??)

American writer

Do I believe I'm blessed? of course I do! In the first place, my mother told me so, many, many times, and when she did, it was always quietly, confidently.

EDWARD KENNEDY "DUKE" ELLINGTON (1894–1974)

American composer, musician and bandleader

GOD IS AS DEPENDENT ON YOU AS YOU ARE ON HIM.

MAHALIA JACKSON (1911–1972)

American singer

If the concept of God has any validity or use, it can only be to make us larger, freer, and more loving.

JAMES BALDWIN (1924–1987)

American writer

NO MATTER WHAT . . . IT IS WITH GOD. HE IS GRACIOUS AND MER-CIFUL. HIS WAY IS THROUGH LOVE IN WHICH WE ALL ARE. IT IS TRULY A—LOVE SUPREME.

JOHN COLTRANE (1926–1967)

American musician and composer

America has abandoned the strong woman of spirituality and is shacking up with the harlot of materialism.

JOSEPH LOWERY (B. 1924)

American cleric

A MAN MUST LIVE IN THE WORLD AND WORK OUT HIS OWN SALVATION IN THE MIDST OF TEMPTATION.

FRANK YERBY (1916–1992)

American writer

One must rise above the earth to become universal.

JEAN TOOMER (1844–1967)

American writer

I'M IN THIS WORLD, AND WHEN I'M GONE I SHALL BECOME A PART OF THE WORLD.

STERLING DOMINIC PLUMPP (B. 1940)

American artist and educator

I'm raising some real hard issues. I don't care about our socio-psychological history as the descendants of slaves. All I want to know is: Black man and woman, do you know God, and why are you still asking someone to free you?

IYANLA VANZANT (B. 1956)

American-born Yoruba priestess and writer

[T]he Negro experience has bred something mystical and strangely different in the Negro soul.

ALAIN LOCKE (1886–1954)

American writer

Unless the image of God be obliterated from the soul, all men cherish the love of liberty.

HENRY H. GARNET (1815–1882)

American educator, former slave, abolitionist, and diplomat

YOUR WEALTH CAN BE STOLEN, BUT THE PRECIOUS RICHES BURIED DEEP IN YOUR SOUL CANNOT.

MINNIE RIPERTON (1947–1979)

American singer

My inner life is mine, and I shall defend and maintain its integrity against all the powers of Hell.

JAMES WELDON JOHNSON (1871–1938)

American writer, educator, and social activist

O God, give me the words to make my dream-children live.

JOSEPH SEAMON COTTER, JR. (1895–1919)

American poet and playwright

UNDERSTANDING THE PAST

MANY OF THE MESSAGES IN THIS BOOK ARE concerned with the future, fulfillment of dreams, or struggling toward goals that may seem elusive. Here, the emphasis is on the past. History is a means of anticipating the future, and a method of understanding the cultural origins of all humankind.

The idea that history is a process, or a line that stretches clearly from beginning to end, is expressed by different speakers. Some remind us that there is no escaping the past and little dignity in trying to escape.

A fool who forgets the past is destined to repeat it. Given the bitter history of black people, it's no wonder that the speakers here want us to remember our history so that others can't ignore it, or call it a lie or an exaggeration.

It's painful to remember a time when people of different cultures didn't get along, but the speakers in this section turn our attention to the past for a reason: They remind us that bad times will surely come again if we ever forget the damage that was done, and they encourage us to remember good times too, in order to keep memories alive in our hearts.

IF THE HOUSE IS TO BE SET IN ORDER, ONE CANNOT BEGIN WITH THE PRESENT; HE MUST BEGIN WITH THE PAST.

JOHN HOPE FRANKLIN (B. 1915)
American historian and educator

There is no way to look at the past. Don't hide from it. It will not catch you if you don't repeat it.

PEARL BAILEY (1918—1990)
American singer

IF YOU UNDERSTAND THE BEGINNING AS WELL, THE END WILL NOT TROUBLE YOU.

ASHANTI PROVERB

By and by when the morning comes
all the saints of God are gathered home
We'll tell the story of how we overcame
for we'll understand it better by and by.
AFRICAN-AMERICAN SPIRITUAL

[H]ISTORY HAS BECOME LESS A MATTER OF ARGUMENT AND MORE A MATTER OF RECORD. THERE IS THE DESIRE AND DETERMINATION TO HAVE A HISTORY, WELL DOCUMENTED, WIDELY KNOWN . . . AND ADMINISTERED AS A STIMULATING AN INSPIRING TRADITION FOR FORTHCOMING GENERATIONS.
ARTHUR SCHOMBURG (1874—1938)
American archivist and banker

I'm not afraid of tomorrow because I've seen yesterday and yesterday is beautiful.
JANET HARMON WATERFORD BRAGG (B. 1907)
American nurse and aviator

WE HAVE A WONDERFUL HISTORY BEHIND US . . . WE ARE GOING BACK TO THAT BEAUTIFUL HISTORY AND IT IS GOING TO INSPIRE US TO GREATER ACHIEVEMENTS.
CARTER G. WOODSON (1875—1950)
American historian

We Black folk, our history and present being, are a mirror of all the manifold experiences of America. What we want, what we represent, is what America is. . . . The differences between Black folk and White folk are not blood or color, and the ties that bind us are deeper than those that separate us.

RICHARD WRIGHT (1908—1960)
American writer

HISTORIES ARE IMPORTANT 'CAUSE THEY POINT THE DIRECTION OF TRADITIONS.

NIKKI GIOVANNI (B. 1943)
American poet, writer, and educator

Black people must learn to look at the past honestly, studying those attributes, both good and bad, which makes us human.

RAY ARANHA (B. 1939)
American actor and playwright

THEY SAY YOU SHOULD NOT SUFFER THROUGH THE PAST. YOU SHOULD BE ABLE TO WEAR IT LIKE A LOOSE GARMENT, TAKE IT OFF AND LET IT DROP.

EVA JESSYE
American choral director

Where there is shame, there is no honor.
GAMBIAN PROVERB

THE TREE CANNOT STAND WITHOUT ITS ROOTS.
ZAIRIAN PROVERB

I never forget for a day, or for an hour, or for a minute, that I climbed to my position on the back of the courageous African-American men and women who went before me.

COLIN L. POWELL (B. 1937)
American military officer and former chairman of Joint Chiefs of Staff

THOSE WHO ARE DEAD ARE NEVER GONE; THEY ARE IN THE THICKENING SHADOWS.
AFRICAN POEM

They recreated history, giving it life through the words and voices.
KENYAN PROVERB

We've got to write our history in reference to the positiveness, because you can't love yourself unless you know that somebody that looks like you has done something special.

OPHELIA DEVORE-MITCHELL (B. 1923)
American model

IT IS ONLY WHAT IS WRITTEN UPON THE SOUL OF MAN THAT WILL SURVIVE THE WRECK OF TIME.
FRANCIS GRIMKE (1850—1937)
American cleric and writer

I found out that the history-whitening process either had left out great things that Black men had done, or that great Black men had gotten whitened.

EL-HAJJ MALIK EL-SHABAZZ [MALCOLM X] (1925—1965)
American cleric and civil rights activist

HISTORY, LIKE BEAUTY, DEPENDS LARGELY ON THE BEHOLDER. SO, WHEN YOU READ THAT . . . DAVID LIVINGSTONE DISCOVERED VICTORIA FALLS, YOU MIGHT BE FORGIVEN FOR THINKING THAT THERE WAS NOBODY AROUND THE FALLS UNTIL LIVINGSTONE ARRIVED ON THE SCENE.

DESMOND TUTU (B. 1931)
South African cleric and social activist

This country couldn't call us Africans because if it had, we would have understood some things about ourselves.

SONIA SANCHEZ (B. 1934)
American poet and educator

With courage born of success achieved in the past, with a keen sense of responsibility which we must continue to assume, we look forward to the future, large with promise and hope. Seeking no favors because of our color or patronage because of our needs, we knock at the bar of justice and ask for an equal chance.

MARY CHURCH TERRELL (1863—1954)
American educator, social activist, and writer

[T]here are many in society who exercise toward us benevolent feelings; still (with sorrow we confess it) there are others who make it their business to enlarge upon the least trifle, which tends to the discredit of any person of color; and pronounce anathemas and denounce our whole body for the misconduct of this guilty one. . . .

SAMUEL E. CORNISH (1795—1858) AND JOHN RUSSWORM (1799—1851)
American newspaper editors and founders of first black newspaper

I am a threat to the degree that I'm trying to tell the truth about America.

CORNEL WEST (B. 1953)
American educator and writer

I HAVE NEVER BEEN QUITE ABLE TO RECONCILE THEORY WITH FACT.
JESSE REDMON FAUSET (1882—1961)
American writer

If you're going to play the game properly, you'd better know every rule.

BARBARA JORDAN (B. 1936)
American politician

TO BE FORCED TO EXCAVATE A HISTORY IS ALSO TO REPUDIATE THE CONCEPT OF HISTORY, AND THE VOCABULARY IN WHICH HISTORY IS WRITTEN, FOR THE WRITTEN HISTORY IS, AND MUST BE, MERELY THE VOCABULARY OF POWER.
JAMES BALDWIN (1924—1987)
American writer

I had no idea history was being made. I was just tired of giving up.

ROSA PARKS (B. 1913)
American civil rights activist

HEREIN LIES THE TRAGEDY OF THE AGE: NOT THAT MEN ARE POOR . . . NOT THAT MEN ARE WICKED . . . BUT THAT MEN KNOW SO LITTLE OF MEN.

W. E. B. DU BOIS (1868—1963)
American educator, social reformer, and writer

What we're saying today is that you're either part of the solution or you're part of the problem

ELDRIGE CLEAVER (B. 1935)
American political activist

THE SHIP THAT SAILED UP THE JAMES ON A DAY WE WILL NEVER KNOW WAS THE BEGINNING OF AMERICA, AND, IF WE ARE NOT CAREFUL, THE END.

LERONE BENNETT, JR. (B. 1928)
American historian and scholar

The child standing looks everywhere and often sees naught, but the old man, sitting on the ground, sees everything.

LIBYAN PROVERB

Not to know what one's race has done in former times is to continue always as a child.

CARTER G. WOODSON (1875—1950)

American historian

EXPERIENCE IS A HARD TEACHER. SHE GIVES THE TEST FIRST, THE LESSON AFTERWARDS.

AFRICAN-AMERICAN PROVERB

The ignorant are always prejudiced and the prejudiced are always ignorant.

CHARLES V. ROMAN (1864—1934)

American physician and educator

How can leadership point the forward way that is utterly ignorant to the past?

DRUSILLA DUNJEE HOUSTON (1876—1941)

American scholar and writer

IF PEOPLE ARE INFORMED THEY WILL DO THE RIGHT THING. IT'S WHEN THEY ARE NOT INFORMED THAT THEY BECOME HOSTAGES TO PREJUDICE.

CHARLAYNE HUNTER-GAULT (B. 1942)

American journalist

CHANGES HAVE BEEN MADE. THE PEOPLE WHO WERE QUIET ARE NOW SPEAKING OUT. BUT I REALIZE THAT YOU CANNOT ERASE IN THIRTY YEARS WHAT IT TOOK TWO HUNDRED YEARS TO ESTABLISH.

DAISY BATES (B. 1914)

American journalist and civil rights activist

This Fourth of July is yours, not mine. You may rejoice, I must mourn.

FREDERICK DOUGLASS (C. 1817—1895)

American writer and abolitionist

Each of us has lost something that once gave the world a dimension it will never have again for us, except in memory.

ROBERT HAYDEN (1913—1980)

American poet and playwright

WE HAVE PURSUED THE SHADOW, THEY HAVE OBTAINED THE SUBSTANCE; WE HAVE PERFORMED THE LABOR, THEY HAVE RECEIVED THE PROFITS; WE HAVE PLANTED THE VINES, THEY HAVE EATEN THE FRUITS OF THEM.

MARIA W. STEWART (1803—1879)

American abolitionist and writer

When you narrow your definition to what is convenient, or what is fashionable, or what is expected, what happens is dishonesty by silence.

AUDRE LORDE (1934—1992)

American poet and essayist

[R]aces, like individuals, must stand or fall by their own merit: that to fully succeed they must practice their virtues of self-reliance, self-respect, industry, perseverance, and economy.

PAUL ROBESON (1898—1976)

American singer and actor

INDEX